Choosing
Plan A

Choosing Plan A

A Mother's Adventure with Adoption, Acceptance After Miscarriage, and Acknowledging the Miracle of Children

Cathie Henry Rosado

Mother of one step, two adopted, three natural
in heaven, and four natural on earth

Choosing Plan A

A Mother's Adventure with Adoption, Acceptance After
Miscarriage, and Acknowledging the Miracle of Children

ISBN (Print Edition): 978-1-7362074-0-6

ISBN (Kindle Edition): 978-1-7362074-1-3

Library of Congress Control Number (LCCN): 2020923232

Printed in the United States of America

Published by Cathie Rosado | Landisville, Pennsylvania

Prepared for publication by www.palmtreeproductions.com

To contact the author:

CHOOSINGPLANA.COM

Dedication

To my niece,
Francesca Lou Henry D'Angelo.

Acknowledgments

Thank you, Heavenly Father, for guiding the adventure I call my life and for remaining patient with me through all of the missteps and mess-ups along the way. Thank you for those times when I ignored your still small voice, and you wisely used the louder voice to challenge my plan. "Are you sure that is my will?" Thank you, Jesus, for coming into my heart when I was a young child and helping me stay reasonably within range of the "straight and narrow." Thank you for being the solution to the hurt and brokenness we experience in this fallen world. Thank you, Holy Spirit, for the nudges that have helped me get it right, and I'm sorry for the times I haven't followed the nudge and messed up great opportunities.

Thank you, Jim and Margaret, Sam and Sherlyn, Don and Doris, Jim and Anne, Kurt and Lora, Jack and Sandy, Mary, Steve and Michelle, Hollis and Gloria, Dr. Jessica, Dr. Sharon, Dr. Kara, Dr. Philip, Jeane', Kristin, Jim and our legal adoption team, the many teachers, children's pastors, youth pastors, counselors, the team at Breath of Life Ministries and Elijah House Ministries, and anyone else I'm forgetting who played a role in positively impacting my life and the lives of my children.

Thank you, "Nanny," for the example of a genuine heart of service during your life and for being there in Heaven to receive my little ones. Please tell your parents and grandparents I look forward to meeting them when I get there. Uncle Bill, thank you for being an awesome uncle here on earth, and thank you for inspiring me to think seriously about legacy.

Thank you, "Mom," for the sacrifices you made for me and for putting me in the path of so many amazing people who could speak into my life. Many years ago, when you were worried you wouldn't survive the knee replacement surgery, I told you that either way, you would wake up with new knees and be able to see three grandchildren from me. You opted to wake up on this side and stuck around long enough to see the rest of my children here. While I miss you, I'm sure you are enjoying spending time with the heavenly grandchildren and definitely enjoying those new knees. Give my heavenly crew a hug and a kiss for me.

Thank you, "Dad," for teaching me the value of hard work and determination and for continuing to be involved in my life. Thank you for being the very popular grandpa for my earthly crew. Valerie, thank you for the help with edits for the book. I'm sure we will miss a few, and I'm ok with that because maybe it's God's way of reminding me to remain humble.

Thank you, Joe, for being the best "little" brother a sister could ever ask for. We've had more than our fair share of ups and downs, and it's great to know there is always someone who will have my back. You are my never-ending source of useful (and sometimes just random) knowledge and practical mechanical advice. Yes, you win for the most raw intelligence, stellar memory, and height, but I'm still the oldest.

Thank you to my children's biological mom for choosing life for them. Thank you for entrusting them to me for a season of parenting, and hopefully, you are as proud as I am of the fine adults they have become. There definitely is a benefit to our interesting adoption story and tag team parenting effort since both of us now get to share in the blessing of the grandchildren.

Thank you, Mila and Navo, for turning my world upside down in the most awesome way. I'm so glad I said yes and chose God's Plan A. I can't even begin to tell you or put into words how proud I am of you. I'm glad I've gotten to be one of your moms.

Thank you, Lydia, Caleb, Joshua, and Nathaniel, for arriving on the scene and challenging me in all-new ways. You are each unique and amazing, and I am excited to see how God's call on your lives unfolds.

Thank you, Jose, for your years of military service and for inspiring Mila and Navo to consider military vocations. Thank you for doing your best to be a good dad despite the lack of a good example in your own life.

Thank you, Mark Wellman and Liberator Medical, for having me on the team at Abilities Expos, where I was able to meet David Farber. Thank you, David, for using your gifts and talents for capturing the beauty of God's creation and being in the right place at the right time for God to remind me there is no excuse I could come up with that He can't equip me to overcome.

Thank you, Wendy Walters, for being my cheerleader and publishing guru to get me from the idea of a book to the actual book. It is almost surreal to be launching this into the world, and it is scary and exciting all at the same time, not that much unlike *Choosing Plan A* in the first place.

Praise for Choosing Plan A

When you pick up this book, *Choosing Plan A*, and read the life story of Cathie, it will inspire you to go beyond the comforts of life into a world of great need. You may find yourself thinking more about how you may be able to make a difference in a child's life. Cathie's courage, determination, and perseverance may challenge you to take on a task that is greater than yourself for the good of others. From the very first chapter, her story is fascinating, easy to read, and inspiring. Cathie's love for God and family is a beacon of light for ALL.

ANNE BEILER

Founder of Auntie Anne's Pretzels , Author, Motivational Speaker

What a compelling story of strength and perseverance: choosing to adopt children, literally dropped on Cathie's doorstep, weeks after her wedding, then experiencing the loss of babies through miscarriage, and finally being able to give birth to full-term babies! Yes, I know Cathie Rosado, and she is indomitable. Be inspired and encouraged by her authenticity and unshakeable trust in God and His Word, her deep love for her family, and her strong desire to impact the lives of those around her practically. May your life be touched and challenged as you read *Choosing Plan A*!

DORIS NEFF

Ladies Care Pastor, Worship Center, Lancaster, PA

This book is a heartwarming story of beauty and brokenness, how God can bring joy out of our sorrows and ministry out of our weaknesses. You will be encouraged and challenged to look at your own life and see how you can make a difference for God in this broken world.

REBECCA CRUTTENDEN
Founder of Team Orphans and Clara Cookies

Cathie's book, *Choosing Plan A,* is more than words on a page; it's an invitation to join Cathie on her raw, real, and redemptive journey to motherhood. Although her journey did not fit some fairytale version, it opened her eyes to the story God was writing for her family. The details of her parenting journey had been unfolding long before she was a mom, and it was in those details she said yes to God—yes to *Choosing Plan A*. You'll find yourself discovering more about God's details in your own life as you relate to various parts of Cathie's story. Our stories are written for His Glory, and Cathie tells hers in a way that will inspire you as she honors Him. By *Choosing Plan A*, she embraces the miracle of motherhood exactly how God designed it for her beautiful family.

TABITHA DELLER
Author, Speaker, Teacher

None of us can do everything, but all of us can do something. Sure, that sounds simple, and it is hard to disagree with the sentiment and not feel selfish or uncaring. But how many of us actually embrace the conviction that we both can and should make a tangible, positive difference in a world beyond what brings us and ours immediate comfort or provision? It is impossible to read Cathie's story without being confronted with possibilities of how we can each do *something* that will make the world a little brighter, push the darkness back a little more, and demonstrate how to bring heaven to earth.

WENDY K. WALTERS
Master Coach, Author, Motivational Speaker

I LOOKED FOR
SOMEONE AMONG
THEM WHO WOULD
BUILD UP THE WALL
AND STAND BEFORE
ME IN THE GAP—

—EZEKIEL 22:30a NIV

THEN I HEARD
THE LORD SAYING,
"WHOM SHALL I
SEND? AND WHO
WILL GO FOR US?"

AND I SAID, "HERE
I AM. SEND ME!"

—ISAIAH 6:8 NIV

Contents

IF YOU THINK MY
HANDS ARE FULL,
YOU SHOULD SEE
MY HEART.

—ADOPTION.COM

Preface
God Had a Plan

―――――――――――――――――

I'm sure just about everyone has been at a social gathering and either asked or heard someone ask the question, "How many children do you have?" I have one of those responses that is a little nontraditional and may just start an interesting conversation. "It depends on how you want to count them, but you could get to ten. One step, two adopted, three natural in heaven, and four natural on earth. I've been actively involved in parenting six and currently I better keep track of four on a daily basis to avoid being on the 6:00 news." And to think – none of that was part of my plan for my life. I wasn't even sure I wanted children. God had a different plan. I was in for the adventure of a lifetime.

I have been told many times over the years that I should write a book. That always seemed like such a daunting task. It would definitely take more than just another human telling me I should. I would need it to be a divine directive to get me moving. God generally has His work cut out for Him when pointing me in a direction and getting me to write a book was going to be no different. Knowing how I am, it would have to be very clear to my head and my heart that I was to do this. Step one would be my head. He would have to put me in a place where I would have some time, have some exposure to the intellectual "how to" since I tend not to leap in faith, and a bit of "if that person can do it what's your excuse."

After selling a family business that I had been pouring my heart, soul, and so much time into for twelve years, I suddenly had more time in my schedule. The next two events were nothing short of God saying it's time to do this and thus I sat down at the computer and started typing.

In late May 2018 I received a call from Mark Wellman in California. He needed a mobile rock wall in Chicago and I had the connections to get it. I agreed to drive it out and to help him with the adaptive climbing at the Abilities Expo. We set up the day before the event was to open. Several other vendors had done the same and we had a little time to wander. I happened to notice a booth diagonal from us that had some nice nature photographs. I went over to take a look. A photo of eagles with the overlay of a portion of Isaiah 40:31 caught my attention.

I am fond of eagles and love when I get to see them soaring. I have the option to intentionally travel to the Conowingo Dam in Maryland to see them, but there is something special about seeing them in other places when it is not expected. They have made a resurgence in my area so a few times a year I will see one flying along the Susquehanna River on my way to or from work. On occasion I will see them in other unexpected places almost as if they are acting as God's little messengers and one day saw one flying over my daughter's soccer team as they were having their devotions.

A few years ago I had to set up equipment for an event in Maryland. I had traveled down by myself and the task before me was not going to be easy but was also not impossible. I had done it on my own before. That particular day everything that could go wrong did seem to go wrong. It started when the truck got stuck in the mud. I decided to get the equipment off of the trailer so at least I could get the trailer out of the way. I struggled but successfully rolled the 600 pounds of vinyl the 30 feet into position only to discover that it had not been put away the way we would always do it and I was now going to have to roll it back the 30 feet. I was now running behind and experiencing the pressure of a deadline knowing the state inspector would be coming to make sure everything was set up according to the code. I did not want to inconvenience him and give him an excuse to be unnecessarily difficult with me. As I was standing there feeling like I could simply collapse in a puddle of tears, which I knew would accomplish absolutely nothing, I looked up and saw an eagle fly over. "Ok Lord, I got the message. You have my back and I can do this."

He gives strength to the weary and increases the power
of the weak. Even youths grow tired and weary,
and young men stumble and fall; but those who hope
in the Lord will renew their strength. They will soar on
wings like eagles; they will run and not grow weary, they
will walk and not be faint.

(ISAIAH 40:29-31)

Things started falling into place. Guys came over with a super duty pickup truck and tow strap and pulled the truck from the mud. The inspector called me and talked himself into trusting me and talked himself out of coming to inspect every detail since their prior experience with me had been good. With these issues resolved my stress level came down and my "can do" attitude returned. There was no need for tears, just focus and do what needs to be done.

Standing there in Chicago and seeing the picture of the eagles with the overlay of the Bible verse meant I wanted to find out more about whoever had that booth. Was it just a person selling pictures or would it be the actual photographer and if so what was his or her story? The next morning I met the photographer, David Farber, and not only did he have all of the impressive pictures, he had his book. In talking to him my interest was piqued. He has a story of adoption intermixed with a tragic accident and finding faith. I bought a copy of "As Best I Can – Journeys by Wheelchair by the Grace of God." It would be a few weeks until I would open the book to read it but when I did it kept my attention and I powered through it in one day.

David was almost killed in a motorcycle accident, but miraculously survived. With nothing short of God-given creativity and ingenuity he and some friends developed a way to support his massive camera on his wheelchair, allowing for his one working arm to do the focusing. With his mouth, aided by technology similar to that used by quadriplegics to operate their wheelchair, he could shoot the pictures. His pictures were amazing in their own right, but considering the challenge of overcoming so many obstacles to get them added to my amazement. Here was a guy in a wheelchair who basically was down to one good arm, one good ear, and one good eye who does amazing photography and wrote a book. I kind of lost any excuse I had for not writing a book.

At the same time, with my new found "free time" I was contemplating writing a blog. That sounded like a step up from Facebook posts but not quite as daunting as a book. If God was calling me to write, maybe I could meet Him halfway...as if that ever works. When I saw the announcement for the Release the Writer conference with Wendy Walters in the bulletin at Life Center I thought, well that might be nice. Maybe I could learn a few things about writing for my blog idea and all the stuff about actually publishing a book I could file in my data bank of knowledge for "sometime down the road." I registered for the conference and something in that decision started pouring vast amounts of water onto those seeds that others had tossed onto the ground of my head. The seeds were now pushing their way down into my heart at lightning speed and beginning to germinate. By the time I walked into the conference I knew a book was a real possibility. I was hungry for whatever wisdom Wendy might be able to impart and was going to sit in the front row.

I had never heard of Wendy Walters before. She was well known at Life Center, but I had been there less than a year at that point. I spent many years in another very solid church but their speaker circuit was different so our paths had never crossed. Wendy kicked it into gear using Revelation 12:11 that we shall overcome by the blood of the Lamb and by the word of our testimony.... and what...the word of our testimony. "Your book is the word of your testimony." OK, so maybe writing a book isn't really optional anymore and my head was becoming ok with that. Maybe this is an issue of whether I will be obedient. That obedience thing can still be a challenge so He was still going to have to make it abundantly clear to my heart that this is a mandate. I figured God would solidify it somehow and as always my head was trying to jump ahead to anticipate how He might do that. I'm not sure it will ever sink in that I can't predict what He's going to do next because He's infinitely more creative than me.

As Wendy wrapped up the conference she sang the doxology

Praise God from whom all blessings flow; Praise him, all creatures here below;

Praise him above, ye heavenly host: Praise Father, Son, and Holy Ghost.

That was it....mandate received.

To understand the significance of the doxology in my life we have to jump back in time.

Though I didn't get to see her that often, my maternal grandmother who lived two hours away in New Jersey had a profound impact on my life. The essence of my heritage of faith I trace directly down from her grandfather who served in the battle of Gettysburg in the Civil War and her father who family lore says crafted the cross that hung on the outside of the Episcopalian church building where I saw her humbly serve. She exemplified Colossians 3:23 "Whatever you do, work at it with all your heart, as working for the Lord." She was meticulous with the altar linens and graciously served in the kitchen for "coffee hour." It wasn't so much what she did that heavily impacted me but how she did it. I saw the example of a true servant's heart that was joyous in the serving.

I remember her telling me the story of how her parents had been going to both a protestant and an Episcopalian church for some time. One day the protestant pastor made the statement that unless you hear the gospel with your physical ears you cannot be saved. He was likely speaking from Romans 10:17 where it says "So then faith comes by hearing, and hearing by the word of God." (NKJV). My great grandmother, after whom I was named, was deaf but she could read lips. Apparently the pastor was looking her direction when he uttered those words. She knew what he said and took offense and not surprisingly they never returned to that church. While the story has been shared all the way down to my generation I know I have only heard one side and this side of Heaven I can't hear the other side. I have chosen to give grace to the pastor and perhaps his words were received in a way that was out of context for what he intended. I think we've all had an experience or two where we've said something and it just didn't come out right. We offended while not intending to offend. If I am correct and the pastor was speaking from Romans then I personally like The Passion Translation of that passage much better. "Faith, then, is birthed in a heart that responds to God's anointed utterance of the Anointed One." The heart is where the perception and acceptance of God's truth happens. Physical ears are just one of the senses through which God can deliver truth. An inability to receive truth through one sense does not preclude a person from receiving salvation or being all God created them to be.

Fortunately my great grandparents didn't abandon their faith. They had a relationship with the Episcopalian church and chose to go there. The worship service styles of Episcopalian churches and protestant churches I've attended in modern times are very different and I have often wondered why they would have ended up at the Episcopal church. A "chance" comment by Reverend J. Connor Haynes at St. Mary's Episcopal Church in Burlington, NJ about a connection between the Episcopal church and "Gallaudet" which I recognized as a name associated with a deaf university led me to learn some interesting history.

> The Episcopal Church began ministry among Deaf people more than 150 years ago - when the Rev Thomas Gallaudet began services in sign language in New York City in 1852. St. Ann's church for the Deaf, still very active, is considered the "mother church" of all congregations of Deaf people in the United States. The Rev. Dr. Gallaudet was personally responsible for organizing many more Episcopal deaf congregations throughout the country. It is thought that St. Ann's was the first organized church of Deaf people in any denomination. The Episcopal Church also claims the honor of being first to ordain a Deaf person. The Rev. Henry Winter Syle was ordained in 1876 beginning a long tradition of clergy who are Deaf in the Episcopal church.[1]

Perhaps it was the Episcopalian church's valuing of the deaf population that led my great grandparents to settle there. You can be assured I'll be asking them in Heaven.

When I was young we would go to New Jersey for several summer weekends to visit my grandmother. There was definitely a perk in that across the street was her sister-in-law's house and they had a pool we could use. At home we went to a more charismatic non-denominational protestant church, but with

"Nanny" we went to St. Barnabas Episcopal Church. On the outside of St. Barnabas hung the cross that family lore says was made by her father. The stained glass, ornate woodwork, amazing architecture, religious statues, and intricate paintings made for lots of interesting and beautiful things to look at – far different from the converted gymnasium we were accustomed to. Her church held a high mass that was very ceremonial using incense, candles, and bells. The priest and other ministers were always dressed in formal "religious" attire that to a young child looked inherently uncomfortable in those hot, humid summer months in a non-air-conditioned old building. Much of the scripture and text was sung rather than spoken. The style was so different from our typical Sunday experience. I was taught that differences in style are ok and the most important part for me to pay attention to was whether the priest was speaking Biblical truth. I didn't realize at that tender age just how important learning to look past style and denominational labels is to unity in the body of Christ, but those lessons have served me well in life.

Without fail, every service at St. Barnabas included the doxology and this was the only place I would ever hear it. As an adult the doxology has become almost a symbol of my grandmother and the generational heritage of faith. The association is very strong and it can evoke considerable emotion. God seems to use it like the eagle to periodically send very clear messages.

My natural children arrived years after my grandmother went to heaven. There was no longer a reason to go to St. Barnabas and my children would likely never hear the doxology in our church. My heart's desire has always been that my children will carry on the heritage of faith. Even though I prefer a different style of church service and thus don't attend an Episcopalian church part of me longs for my children to appreciate the liturgical Episcopalian heritage that sustained the family for several generations. In one of those obviously God moments I happened to be sitting in the kindergarten classroom of Veritas Academy, a classical Christian school founded by Presbyterians, waiting to help chaperone a field trip and heard the teacher start singing the doxology with the students. My mascara was being seriously threatened as I realized my children were learning some of the same liturgical things of our heritage of faith and in particular, the doxology. It was as if God was speaking directly to my heart and telling me this is exactly where my children belong.

Now, here I was at the end of a writer's conference in a very non liturgical church and God drives home His message using a very liturgical song with such tremendous personal meaning. To add to the emotion of the moment, during a break earlier in the day I had dialogued with another writer about generational blessings and the heritage of faith that is passed down. During the dinner break I was working on a portion of this book that speaks of my grandmother in a vision. Memories involving my grandmother were in the front of my mind and now the doxology was being sung. I couldn't even get the words out. He had just solidified it in my heart that there was now a mandate to write this book.

Every little girl grows up with a version of the princess story and living happily ever after. I had my plan for my life. I would graduate from college, land a great job, buy my first house, thrive in my career, find and marry prince charming, maybe have children— but not so sure about that one, and live happily ever after in my nice neat happy little world. I was confident that God loved me, so surely He would bless me with my heart's desire. He always has my best interest at heart, and His plan would surely coincide with mine.

I think it's safe to say I had some maturing to do and needed to learn that it's not necessarily all about me. There is a bigger picture, and I'm just one player in that bigger picture. Maybe the bigger picture means I don't get everything I want when I want it. Maybe the bigger picture means I need to be part of someone else's bigger picture.

When I walked across the stage to receive my high school diploma, I was on my path. As far as I was concerned, no guy, much less a baby, would change that. I was singularly focused and would be starting at the Wharton School at the University of Pennsylvania in the fall with the plan of getting a bachelor of science in economics degree with concentrations in accounting and entrepreneurial management.

Less than two hundred miles away, another young woman was on a different path. She was a very young teenager in the clutches of a much, much older man and mother to a six-month-old baby girl. By the time I started school in the fall, she was expecting another child. I'm confident this was not the princess story she had envisioned.

I graduated from college, landed my dream job in Philadelphia, and bought my first house in quiet Lancaster County. I was excelling and starting to get involved with philanthropic endeavors. Miles away, the other young woman was managing toddlers.

I hadn't yet found prince charming, so I added graduate school to the mix. Miles away, the other young woman had two children in early elementary school and another new arrival. She had a new man in her life who was considerably closer to her age. Maybe her life would start looking a little more like her dream. Not even in my wildest dreams could I have ever imagined our paths would cross.

The year 2000 came, and the world had entered a new millennium. For those who lived through that time, we remember there was the question of whether we would survive or if every computer-based thing would crash and somehow, life as we knew it would cease to exist. My life moved into warp speed change, and to some degree, life as I knew it did cease to exist. I changed jobs, finished graduate school, got married, got two children, lost my grandmother, and lost a baby. The other woman's life changed massively that year also. She moved away and left two children behind.

When the phone rang in September 2000, I had a choice to make. Fortunately, lots of seemingly inconsequential influences and events up to that point were pointing me in the right direction. However, I still had a split-second decision to make that could radically change the direction of my life:

WOULD I CHOOSE ADOPTION AS MY PLAN A?

ENDNOTE

1. http://www.ecdeaf.org/about/history-of-ecd/

Chapter 1
The Dogwood Tree

M y very early childhood was in the stereotypical perfect little American family—dad, mom, a little girl, and a little boy living in a nice middle-class home in a quiet little town. It was a beautiful brick home on a nice plot of land surrounded by other well established older homes. Each house had its own unique charm. Some had big front porches while others had stately columns. Ours had a terra cotta roof that would rumble when heavy snow slid off in the winter. The yards afforded plenty of room for children to run and be creative in their play. The only drawback for my brother and me was that there weren't many other children in the area. My brother and I were forced to get along with each other otherwise it would be a pretty lonely existence.

One day our little world got more exciting when a new family moved in next door. Suddenly my brother and I had playmates. The three oldest children, a girl and two boys, were right around our ages. We were all fast friends. We could play fort in the mature trees around our homes and collect the jewel-like sap that oozed out of the cherry tree in our yard. Dried hydrangea flowers made great Special K cereal to mix with rainwater which, if so inclined, we could then "cook" on the hot metal of an old car parked in the back corner of the spacious driveway. A shed-like area on the back of the garage could be our clubhouse. For hours and hours we could play outside creating adventures with our new friends.

There was one thing that made their family a little different than ours. Our three playmates had two younger siblings. These younger siblings had darker skin than everyone else in the family. That never seemed to bother anyone in their family so it never bothered me. I didn't really understand fostering or adopting at that point so while their family didn't look like mine it was ok and I didn't really question it. While it may have seemed different at first it became normal in our little world.

I remember there were several large trees in the front yard of that childhood home. They were quite mature with wide trunks. At times my brother and I would play silly games pretending we could hide from passing cars behind those trunks. One of the trees was an American sweetgum. It would drop its hard dry fruit all over the yard which was likely somewhat annoying when mowing the grass and definitely annoying when they would get caught in the rake when cleaning up fall leaves. We children could have endless hours of fun collecting those "gumballs" and shaking the seeds out of them. They, along with the assorted sizes of pine cones around the property, provided excellent craft materials.

The other two trees suitable for our hiding games were dogwoods. In the spring they would bloom in shades of white and pink. Being brought up in a Christian home they afforded a convenient way for our parents to explain the salvation story using the legend and poem of the dogwood tree. In all likelihood since the dogwood is not native to the Middle East the legend would not be true, but true or not it was a tangible reminder of my faith every spring when the trees would bloom.

The Dogwood Tree
by Anonymous

When Christ was on earth, the dogwood grew
To a towering size with a lovely hue.
Its branches were strong and interwoven
And for Christ's cross its timbers were chosen

Being distressed at the use of the wood
Christ made a promise which still holds good:
"Not ever again shall the dogwood grow
To be large enough for a tree, and so

Slender and twisted it shall always be
With cross-shaped blossoms for all to see.
The petals shall have bloodstains marked brown
And in the blossom's center a thorny crown.

All who see it will think of Me,
Nailed to a cross from a dogwood tree.
Protected and cherished this tree shall be
A reflection to all of My agony."

There was something extra special about one of our dogwood trees. One of the trees bloomed with two different colors. Some of the branches were white and some were pink. I remember my mother explaining that somewhere along the line the branches had been grafted. A small branch from another tree was taken off and put on this one to make it a multi-colored tree. That was an interesting proposition. Branches from another tree being joined together to make a single tree. Did God intend that Dogwood tree with its multi-colored branches to foreshadow the story of my family tree?

I've done a little reading on grafting and I don't know if the tree was technically grafted or if it was created using the budding process. As best as I can tell in grafting one generally plans for an optimal situation when a plant is dormant. You trim the two branches connecting them perfectly and control the environment so they can join together. In the other process of budding, which is apparently easier and doesn't require the perfectly controlled environment, you insert a bud under the bark of the recipient tree. The bud will grow into a new branch with characteristics of the original plant.

Some families choose to adopt when there has been a period of dormancy in their quest to grow their family. Some families add a budding newborn while others graft in a branch of an older child or sibling group. Some families choose to sequester their family away in the perfect environment for a season to allow their new family to bond and others just have to navigate their way through everyday life. Some have done extensive planning to prepare for the growth of their family while others, because of a crisis situation, may be thrust into the growth of a family with little or no time to prepare.

The academic in me would love to be able to draw a perfectly clear parallel with my children and the process in the natural tree. As nice as that idea sounds I think I've had to accept that it is next to impossible. There is no "one-process-fits-all" in real life. For us it was the furthest thing from a perfectly stable pristine controlled environment into which we brought an eight and nine-year-old sibling group. We didn't have time to consciously plan or prepare and our lives were anything but dormant. It was early in the school year and we had full-time jobs. Bonding would just have to happen in amongst everyday life.

While reading about the natural trees I found the quote "budding is quicker and usually gives a much better yield than propagating from seeds."[1] Considering I was thinking about my own story I had to laugh. One cannot deny that Mila and Navo showed up quicker than natural children. My attempts at natural children took many years and had a 57% success rate. In my case "grafting" in children was quicker and did give a much better yield rate than "propagating from seed."

A natural gardener draws on all of his knowledge and experience with different techniques to craft a creative tree like those childhood dogwoods. The Master Gardner used His knowledge and experience with different techniques to creatively craft my family tree. While at times it didn't seem like it, He knew exactly what He was doing. The end result is a beautiful multi-colored tree.

Looking at nature can provide other interesting parallels with the development of our family tree. Our family tree was subjected to a variety of stressors and thus didn't exactly grow perfectly. I once caught a piece of a television program about gentleman who go hunting for trees with burls. "A burl results from a tree undergoing some form of stress ... Burls yield a very peculiar and highly figured wood, prized for its beauty and rarity."[2] If I could see our family as a natural tree I'm sure there would be some big burls on it. We definitely endured periods of significant stress and as painful and challenging as those times were they have created some rare beauty in the form of resilience and fortitude.

The periods of stress also forced me to push roots down deep into my faith. I needed deep roots to keep from being toppled and destroyed when the storms came.

> *"But blessed is the one who trusts in the Lord, whose confidence is in Him. They will be like a tree planted by the water that sends out its roots by the stream. It does not fear when heat comes; its leaves are always green. It has no worries in a year of drought and never fails to bear fruit."*
>
> JEREMIAH 17:7-8

I can't say my natural mind was without fear or worries at all times. There were many challenging days in my journey into motherhood. I also didn't always bear sweet, beautiful fruit. There were times of deformed, smelly, rotting fruit, but for all of the mess-ups and failures the good fruit remains. On those roughest, hottest days the roots did find the water in the fountain of God's truth.

ENDNOTES

1. Retrieved from https://sites.psu.edu/buddingdogwoods/2014/04/06/hello-world/.
2. Retrieved from https://en.wikipedia.org/wiki/Burl.

Chapter 2
Activism

Roe v. Wade was decided in 1973, the year I was born.
Abortion became a hot topic. The country became divided
down the line of pro-choice or pro-life. That same year the
National Right to Life Committee was formally incorporated and
grassroots organizations began popping up around the nation.
One particular couple was among the forerunners and has had a
lasting impact in my life.

Jim and Anne Pierson started a home for young unwed mothers
in the early 1970s as an outgrowth of their work with youth in
Washington DC. They were pioneers in the idea of having a
family model for maternity homes with live-in house parents
providing strong mentoring examples and guidance for young
unwed mothers. By the latter part of the 1970s they had started
a houseparent run maternity home in Lancaster County, PA. By
1984 they had moved into authoring materials and mentoring
those on the front lines of pro-life ministry.

Jim and Anne were members of my home church and on Sanctity of Human Life Sundays would regularly raise awareness to pro-life issues. They have a special needs daughter and truly walked out being pro-life with her. They were consistent and genuine in their pro-life position both in their professional and personal lives. They were a living example that being pro-life wasn't just words from a platform but a true way of life.

I volunteered at times for their ministry and got to know their daughter. I knew them on a first name basis and could easily be on the receiving end of a bear hug from Jim. The pro-life agenda wasn't just something in politics or Washington DC. It had a local face.

In 1985 Dr. John Willke became the voice of a radio show called Pro-Life Perspectives which aired in various areas around the country. It aired on the local radio station, WJTL. From age twelve until I headed off to college I heard the regular radio broadcasts and became educated in the topics of the pro-life movement. I had very definite opinions and strong convictions on pro-life issues. I staunchly believed that life starts at conception and thus abortion was taking a human life. I knew that around 6 weeks the baby's heart begins to beat and by 10 weeks they have little fingers and little toes. I even had a definitive moral position on every form of birth control based on the underlying science and whether that birth control prevented conception or prevented implantation. With knowledge comes responsibility and I took that responsibility seriously. On a personal level I would not waiver on those convictions.

I also understood that if one would not stand for abortion there had to be an option for the woman who did not want to parent her child. I didn't know what it would be like to walk in the shoes of a woman facing tough decisions around an unwanted pregnancy yet I held strong opinions. I was a strong supporter of adoption. Putting a child up for adoption was obviously a far better choice than ending the life of the child. I strongly believed Christians should adopt these children. The pastor of my church was a great example in this regard and one of his daughters was adopted. I also saw examples of unofficial adoptive type arrangements in my extended family. A mother had walked out of her child's life and a sister-in-law stepped in to assist with parenting the daughter left behind. Grandparents reared a granddaughter because their daughter was so young when the baby was born.

It is very easy to have strong beliefs on a topic if it doesn't directly impact you on a personal level. I was very pro-adoption... but for someone else. Adoption surely wasn't in any of my plans for me personally.

I remember hearing many sermons growing up which would mention James 1:27 and our responsibility "to look after orphans and widows in their distress." It wasn't a "maybe if you feel like it you could." It was part of the "religion that God our Father accepts as pure and faultless."

I suppose it is no coincidence that verse 27 comes right after another group of verses.

> Do not merely listen to the word, and so deceive yourselves. Do what it says. Anyone who listens to the word but does not do what it says is like someone who looks at his face in a mirror and, after looking at himself, goes away and immediately forgets what he looks like. But whoever looks intently into the perfect law that gives freedom, and continues in it—not forgetting what they have heard, but doing it—they will be blessed in what they do.
>
> JAMES 1:22-25.

It looks to be pretty clear. Do what the word of God tells us to do which is to look after the orphans. Of course there are many ways to meet the needs of orphans. Mailing a check to a ministry on the front lines qualifies. Packing meals destined for distribution to orphans qualifies. I could easily handle those things. In my calculation these things would qualify for the promise at the end that if we are obedient we will be blessed. It's easy to like those verses about being blessed.

SURELY GOD ONLY EXPECTED MY CONVENIENT GIFT—HE WOULDN'T EXPECT MORE THAN JUST SHALLOW ACTION, WOULD HE?

I had my mind made up that I would support the causes that helped the orphans and widows because obviously that was the right thing to do and carried the promise of a blessing. Surely I could very easily squeeze doing the right thing into my life without much challenge. Surely God only expected my convenient gift. Surely He wouldn't expect more than just shallow action. Someone else could be compelled into action that requires sacrificial obedience and I would gladly cheer them on.

By my mid-20s I had completed college and had a good job. I was still single and felt strongly that some of my financial blessings and talent should be invested in pro-life ministries. I developed relationships with all of the various ministries around Lancaster. It was not uncommon for me to be in their offices or having lunch with their directors. I even stepped on to the board of a Christian home for unwed mothers.

All of these activities were great and I was adding value, but there was still a piece that was missing. It's very easy to give lip service to what we believe. It was easy for me to write a check, go to a board meeting, or even make a referral. None of those things really demanded much of me. None of those things took me outside of my comfort zone. None of those were truly sacrificial at a level that impacted my comfortable lifestyle.

I vividly remember visiting Mom's House in Lancaster, a facility that provides daycare support to single moms who are completing an educational or vocational program. It was just a typical day and a typical visit. As I was standing there chatting with the staff a mother came in with her child. Mom had some things to take care of and someone asked if I would hold her little boy. Sure, that was no big deal. He was a cute little guy and probably somewhere between a year and 18 months of age. He happened to be African American. I can't tell you what it was about that interaction on that fateful day but as I stood there holding him God definitively planted the seed for adoption in my heart. It was as if God was speaking very directly into my heart that not only could I adopt, but I could adopt across culture and outside of my plain vanilla looks.

At the time I was still single and the thought of children still seemed very far away. I don't know exactly when that interaction happened but it was somewhere between late 1995 and early 1997.

"Where your treasure is, there your heart will be also." (Matthew 6:21) The verse is right after "Do not store up for yourselves treasures on earth, where moths and vermin destroy, and where thieves break in and steal. But store up for yourselves treasures in heaven, where moths and vermin do not destroy, and where thieves do not break in and steal." (Matthew 6:19-20) It speaks of the treasures in heaven which come from using our time, talents, and financial blessings to serve Christ while here on this earth.

If I strip verse 21 down to a very simple level and propose my own translation, "where your money is, there your heart will go." If I have a lot of money tied up in my car or my house I will probably care a great deal about those things. If I have a lot of money tied up in jewelry or hobbies I will probably care a great deal about those things. I believe your heart follows your cash. In choosing to invest my money in pro-life ministries my heart actively followed. As my heart followed so did my commitment of the treasure of my time to support the ministries. On some level my own actions were unconsciously preparing my heart and watering those seeds of adoption that God had planted. Where my money had gone my life was soon to go.

WHERE YOUR
TREASURE IS,
THERE WILL YOUR
HEART BE ALSO.

MATTHEW 6:21

Chapter 3
Welcome to Marriage and Parenthood

On July 15, 2000, I walked down the aisle of a church thinking the next part of my fairy tale would begin. I was getting married and would live happily ever after. The foreshadowing of what was to come was there but I didn't realize just how quickly the foreshadowing would become my reality.

In 1999 my fiancé's sister was a single mom with two sons and three daughters still at home. They ranged in age from nine to mid-teens. She and the children had been staying with her oldest daughter and her family. Her daughter had two children from a prior relationship and one to her current boyfriend. Three adults and eight children in one house trying to make it on two small incomes was not a recipe for success. The situation was not working out and it was necessary for my fiancé's sister and five children to find a new living arrangement. With no money and no job finding a place to go was not going to be easy. The easiest option was to show up on the porch of her brother's four-bedroom house. Perhaps he would take her in.

I wasn't particularly stressed about the idea because the plan after we got married was for him to move into my house. We could realistically afford to help her get on her feet and she and the children could continue to stay at the house for a while even after we got married. It wasn't necessary for us to sell his house right away. My giving heart was ready to help and we went out shopping for bunk beds, mattresses, and comforters. It was a little chaotic in the house but at least his sister, nieces and nephews had a roof over their heads and places to sleep.

By February 2000 my fiance's niece and her boyfriend were considering moving to New York City. One weekend they dropped off the two oldest children, her children from a previous relationship. They headed to New York with their toddler daughter. His niece didn't return after the weekend. More days and weeks passed and she did not return. I don't think any of us wanted to admit it but we all knew she wasn't coming back. An eight-year-old boy and nine-year-old girl were now unofficially in the care of their grandmother.

On Sunday mornings we would load up two cars and take the whole group along with us to church. Three adults and seven children ages eight to the middle teens was quite the entourage. I was the only one who had really grown up in a church and remained consistent into adulthood. For everyone else this was all quite new.

Sometimes after church I would stick around the house and watch the children so my fiancé's sister could run a few errands or get things done without lots of distractions. I would put the veggie tales videos in the VCR for them to watch and was starting to have my sheltered belief that everyone knows the basic Bible stories shattered. They didn't understand that many of the videos were creative interpretations of Bible stories just using assorted vegetables as the characters. One day we saw a rainbow in the sky and I asked them if they had ever heard of the story of Noah. The fact that Easter was just about a bunny and Christmas was just Santa meant I should have known the answer before I asked the question.

> ONE DAY WE SAW A RAINBOW IN THE SKY AND I ASKED THEM IF THEY HAD EVER HEARD OF THE STORY OF NOAH

I was developing a relationship with all of the children, but was taking particular interest in the two youngest. There was a piece of me that could identify with them even if it was only a very small piece on a very small scale. I remember one weekend when I was about their age miscommunication between my parents landed me at my grandparents' house. School was out for the summer and my brother and I were living with our dad. My parents had recently separated and my mother was trying to find a place to live where we could come stay with her. My dad took off to the beach for the weekend and the young neighbor guy across the street, at most in his early 20s, was supposed to watch us until our mother finished work and came to get us. As it got later into the evening and my mother still had not come this poor young man was at a loss for what to do. We didn't have cell phones back then and the only phone number we had for my mother was her office phone number. It was well past 5:00 and she was no longer at the office and wouldn't be back until Monday. We didn't know where the apartment was that she had just moved into and the young man didn't have a car to try to drive us even if we had known where the apartment was. I'm sure he didn't want to be responsible for two children for the whole weekend. He knew our paternal grandparents lived at the other end of town and that became his best option. He was able to get them on the phone and they agreed that we could come stay there. We gathered some things and walked the mile down the road to their house.

I tried calling my dad's girlfriend's house but of course she was out of town with him. I tried calling her parents' house but they had no way to reach my dad either. My paternal grandparents didn't have a car so we were definitely there until a parent came for us.

My grandparents were not used to having children around for anything more than short visits. They had struggled financially over the years and couldn't afford the greatest dental care. They had lost all of their teeth years earlier so what food they had would be things they could handle "chewing." I think my brother and I were sustained for the weekend on chicken noodle soup from a can, spaghetti o's from a can, ring bologna, bread with butter sprinkled with granulated sugar, and ice cream. It was definitely not the epitome of great nutrition for growing children, but beat the alternative of going hungry. I'm sure on some level the ice cream and the bread with sugar were pleasurable for our taste buds.

It was the longest weekend of my life. There weren't that many child-friendly options to pass the time. We could sit in the house and watch TV or we could sit on the front porch watching cars go by, which was a common pastime for my grandparents. I remember sitting on the front steps for much of Saturday watching up and down the road hoping I would see my mom's car appear but it didn't. It seemed like an eternity until Sunday night came and my dad returned from the beach and got the message that we were at his parents' house.

While I could not completely understand what these two young children were going through having mom walk out of their life there was a part of me that understood just a tiny little bit of what it's like to long for the return of a parent.

As time passed I became concerned about some of the practical things in the children's care and knew at some point they would need some stability. One day I actually called an attorney who was recommended by one of my pro-life ministry contacts. I inquired as to what would be involved if someday down the road someone were to want to adopt them. He gave me the answers and I filed them away for future reference. I think subconsciously I knew I was calling with the idea that it might be me who would adopt them, but I had a wedding to plan so adopting children was definitely not on the immediate list of things to do.

The wedding day came and family and friends joined us. Running around in the background were two little children.

Sunday evenings at my mother-in-law's apartment were a tradition. Any of the seven brothers and sisters and their families may drop in for coffee or rice and beans. We were married just a few weeks and had taken all of the children with us to visit her. During that visit we realized that the situation with the children was deteriorating and deteriorating badly. There was no way my sister-in-law could handle the seven children on her own. The two youngest were going to need a new home and very soon.

I had left my corporate job in early 2000 to work at the church we were attending and where we had just held the wedding. I was part of the hand-picked team of the relatively new senior pastor. It was an ambitious team. Things were going well. The church was growing and we were rapidly retiring debt that had burdened the congregation for years. I was in charge of installing the new software system for the church and bringing the financial systems up to a level of excellence consistent with what one might find in the corporate world.

While I was at my mother-in-law's apartment Sunday night learning that the children's housing situation was in trouble, the senior pastor was preaching what would become his last sermon at the church. He and the board did not agree on the direction for the congregation and by the end of Monday the church was heading for a split as our leader was told to leave.

I so badly wanted to throw my keys on the table and walk out, but the pastor who had hired each of us told us not to leave until we felt God released us to leave. Whenever that time came we were told we should leave with honor. He would not tolerate us making a rash, selfish decision out of anger at what had happened to him. He did not want us to create any further damage for the people in the church. That was tough direction to hear but was absolutely the right thing to tell us.

Just days later my office phone rang. It was Thursday afternoon at 4:00 and I was being told that Children and Youth had stepped into my sister-in-law's situation and was holding the two youngest children at the elementary school. It was decision time. Were we willing to take them? If we didn't take them, Children and Youth would just put them into the foster care system.

"For out of the abundance of the heart the mouth speaks" (Luke 6:45b). All of that pro-life education and the seeds of adoption were in my heart. Out of the abundance of my heart my mouth spoke. "Yes, we will take Mila and Navo." I immediately headed to the school and by 6:00 I was standing in my kitchen trying to figure out what to feed them for dinner.

We still hadn't fully combined our houses and my kitchen definitely didn't have "child friendly" food options like chicken nuggets or hot dogs. As I started going through what I could scrounge together that might be remotely "child-friendly" one child was ok with ravioli and the other child was ok with spaghetti. There would be no settling on just one option so yes, I prepared two different things that night.

Mila and Navo literally arrived with just the clothes on their backs. Those clothes needed to be burned. We headed out to the mall and I found a store that had children's clothes. I walked in having absolutely no idea what I was doing. I looked at the children and asked them what size they wore. Navo piped up and said size 4. Ok, I don't know any better. I went to the rack and picked up a shirt that was size 4. It looked rather small. I then resorted to trying to find a tag in the collar of his shirt. I had no such luck. The printing was completely worn away. I looked at the clerk and asked if she had any idea what size they might wear. She looked at me as if I was a little too clueless and asked me how old they were. I answered 8 and 9. She responded back that I should try 8-10. Oh, there's a logic to this. We managed to find something that they could wear for school the next day and then headed home.

When I bought my house in 1995 I arranged the "three" bedrooms as one for me, one for a small office, and one for a guest room. It may have been a bit of divine preparation that I had set the guest room up with two single day beds and thus I already had beds for two children.

The next morning it was time to scramble to get myself ready for work and then get two children up and off to school. A debate ensued on whether they should get a bath or a shower and I started emotionally falling apart. The reality of the responsibility of two children and absolutely no clue what I was doing was setting in. I think we decided on baths because that's what the children said they wanted and would keep me from drowning in a torrent of tears. Somehow I got them to school and headed to the office.

As I walked into the office I looked at two of the moms on the staff and said "you and you, my office, now!" I desperately needed a crash course in parenting and I started the interrogation. "What time do they get up? What time do they go to bed? What do they eat? What do you do with them on the weekend?"

It wasn't like I had any time to prepare or read up on parenting. This wasn't a case of nine months to prepare. This wasn't even a case of taking an adoption class and being on a waiting list. I was an instant parent and by 3:00 two children would be back in my custody again. I would have to get all the way through the weekend before the next break of dropping them off at school on Monday morning. Much of that first weekend became an adventure in shopping at consignment stores to build a wardrobe of clothing and shopping at the grocery store to find food they would eat.

One of the recommendations for the weekends was the park. "Ok, park, got it. I can do that." I'll never forget taking them to the East Lampeter Park a few weeks into our adventure as a family. They were chasing each other around the playground while I was standing there having a casual conversation with a mom. One of them came running up to me screaming "mommy, mommy." I must have frozen and turned pale because the other woman looked at me and asked "are you ok?" All I could muster was "I'm not sure what to do with that term." She asked, "Oh, are you a foster mom?" I didn't know how to answer her other than to say "I feel like a glorified babysitter who doesn't get to take them home." I was filling the role of mom, but I hadn't yet settled into that role within my own head and heart. I was living some kind of surreal existence. When I had first talked to the attorney about the possibility of adopting it sounded like such a noble idea. With two children now in front of me the weight of the responsibility was becoming real. Maybe it wasn't going to be as carefree as that romanticized image I had in my head.

Chapter 4
Navigating the System

I grew up in a home where mom worked and medical insurance was taken care of through employers. We may not have had much but what we had she worked to purchase. While dad didn't live with us anymore he had a small business with employees and medical insurance was available for his employees and their families. I had no concept of social services and government systems. In my mind those were reserved for the neediest of the population or for whom circumstances had been particularly bleak and temporary support was needed while they got back on their feet.

When Mila and Navo landed in our laps we couldn't just put them on our medical insurance at our employers because they weren't our natural children or legally adopted children. We would need something to fill the gap until we might legally adopt them. I remember getting a call from the social worker who asked whether we would need Christmas presents for the children. He could easily help us through the Toys for Tots program. I assured him that since these were the first two grandchildren in the family Christmas presents would be easily taken care of without assistance but what I could use help with was medical insurance.

We were not technically foster parents so there was no financial assistance coming our way. These were basically our children who were our sole responsibility but without the ability to get the support of typical benefits through employers. He informed me that I would have to contact the welfare office, but he still seemed much more concerned about the Christmas presents and asked again about those. I was so frustrated. Where are the priorities? Needs or wants? We had already been through giving Mila her first real birthday party which totally overwhelmed her. She barely understood "wants" and for Christmas was asking for new underwear. In my world new underwear is just something we go out and buy. That's not a Christmas present. Christmas would be a time for her to dream – of course within some level of reason. I saw the social worker's role to be helping me with the critical needs and I felt like he wasn't getting it. I've come to realize that we weren't the typical extended family placement. I also learned a few months later that our file was closed and sent to Harrisburg. There were so many other much more dysfunctional cases to follow-up on and thus we could be considered "case closed."

It seemed so bizarre to be calling the welfare office as an Ivy League-educated, employed person, but it would be the hoop I would need to jump through for now. The woman on the other end of the phone informed me that I would have to complete some paperwork and should come down to the office and wait in line. I clarified my understanding that all I really needed to do was complete some paperwork and then asked to have it mailed to me. She said she couldn't do that. I would need to come to the office. I assured her that if I had questions on the paperwork I would call or stop in but would really appreciate it if she could just drop the forms in the mail. Apparently it was not in her regular routine to mail out forms and she wasn't going to budge. I was getting rather irritated so felt compelled to resort to logic and my position of authority. I asked her if she was a government employee to which she responded that she was. I then asked whether that meant she was paid for by tax dollars and she agreed. I then informed her that since I was an employed person who pays taxes I thus pay her salary which means she works for me and she could put the forms in an envelope and mail them to me. If necessary I would mail in payment for the stamp. Apparently I was successful at making my point and a few days later the forms arrived in my mailbox.

In some ways it was amusing completing the forms. There were questions about whether I owned a house or rented and whether I had a car or took public transportation. It asked how many children I had and whether I was still of childbearing age. I was guessing they were gathering data for the budget for the next eighteen years and beyond. Considering any natural born children could be placed on the insurance available to me at my employer I felt I could realistically skip some of the questions. At face value it made no sense that we should be accepted for governmental insurance for the children but they weren't yet legally our children so it was the only option available. Children and Youth hadn't done anything to get us legal rights for the children so we would have to use these governmental services until we could have our own attorney privately work through all of the legal rights issues.

I was accustomed to dental visits every six months and asked the children when they had last been to the dentist. I received a blank look. One of the challenges in the early days was that they often didn't understand the words I used. I couldn't say stop disobeying me because they didn't know the word disobey. I had to bring everything down to the simplest language so "stop being bad." After the blank look to the dentist question I realized they didn't know what a dentist was. I went on to describe a dentist as a doctor who plays around in your mouth. The blank look continued so I guessed that they hadn't been to one or at least not recently enough to remember.

Their biological mom had left their birth certificates and immunization records behind but beyond that I really had no idea of their history and unfortunately an eight and nine-year-old really can't answer much. They didn't come with a "handbook of medical history." I didn't know the medical history of their parents. I could piece together some of the history of extended relatives on the maternal side but absolutely nothing on their father's side.

A form came home from the public school about a dental bus or something coming to the school. I signed the form and made a special request to give me direct feedback since I had no idea what their dental situation might be. The feedback was that everything was fine. (I think that person may have barely passed dental hygienists' school.) I was somewhat encouraged but still opted to head down the path of getting them in for routine dental visits because that's just what you do in my world.

I called my dentist and their recommendation was to consider a pediatric dentist since the children had no experience around a dentist. I started looking through the phone book for pediatric dentists. I called the first one and they asked what insurance we had. When I mentioned the government program they informed me that they didn't accept that and I should try somewhere else. After about the third call I was catching on to a pattern. No one accepted that insurance. The next pediatric office I called was in an ideal location for us. Of course, the woman on the other end of the phone informed me that they did not take that insurance. She was ready to hang up but I asked her to stay on the line for a minute. "I'm guessing there's a good reason that no one accepts this insurance and I'm guessing it has to do with reimbursement levels or a lack thereof."

"Correct," she confirmed, then explained that in an example of filling a cavity, government insurance barely covered the cost of the materials for the filling. The office would receive nothing for the labor time of the dentist or assistants let alone the lights and other overhead costs. As a business person, I would not want to accept patients with that insurance either. I then asked if I walked in and put cash on the counter would the dentist look at my children's teeth and tell me if we have issues that need to be addressed. She put me on hold and headed off to check with the dentist who owned the practice. "Good news!" she returned to the line, "Our team will help you."

AS A BUSINESS PERSON, I WOULD NOT WANT TO ACCEPT PATIENTS WITH THAT INSURANCE EITHER

That first visit became one of assessing the situation, prioritizing what was needed, and laying out the costs of each item on what would become our "to do" list. We could now start knocking off items on the "to do" list as cash became available. Around $1,500 later we had tackled the assorted cavities, resolved the critical problems, and put preventative measures in place.

I definitely learned a lot about navigating the governmental systems for medical insurance and was quite happy when we could get out of them. Amusingly it took several years after their legal adoption before I was able to get the welfare office to cease mailing me an annual application for governmental insurance.

Chapter 5
The Fairy Tale is Falling Apart

W hen I got married I was already 27. I felt the biological clock was ticking and opted to let nature run its course. The fact that two children had now showed up 10 weeks into marriage sort of made me start rethinking that "nature run its course" plan. Given my position on birth control options based on the science I learned from Dr. Willke, this wasn't going to be a quick and easy decision.

On November 1, my maternal grandmother passed away. She was supposed to come out to visit us the following weekend but a massive heart attack dropped her instantly on the kitchen floor of her home. She had the early signs of congestive heart failure and Alzheimer's, but we did not expect this. She was the symbol of my spiritual heritage and while she was the grandparent who lived the farthest distance from us she was the one I most revered.

The family desperately needed some good news and my brother and his wife planned to announce they were expecting a child.

As my mother and I drove to the funeral in New Jersey she said she thought for sure my husband and I would go first since we were older. I joked "you never know, I could get pregnant and go early." What I didn't realize at that moment was that I actually was pregnant.

Within a few weeks I realized I was pregnant and was immediately overwhelmed. I was only weeks into parenting an 8 and 9-year-old. I did not feel at all ready to add a baby to the mix. I was still adjusting to being married and this new role of parenting children. At least these children could follow verbal direction and be somewhat self-sufficient. How in the world could I be ready in nine months to add a completely dependent child into the mix? It was too late to change anything now and I wouldn't be able to hide it forever.

On Christmas morning I handed my mother a small jewelry box. As she opened the lid she saw tiny hands and tiny feet pins. She instantly recognized that jewelry. The pins were the exact size of the hands and feet of a 10-12 week old baby in utero and were quite popular among pro-life women. She was elated beyond belief. She now had two baby grandchildren on the way.

To put it mildly Mila was less than excited. We had already been struggling with some of her outbursts as she started venting off the stuff that was bottled up inside and news of a baby was likely going to escalate the unpleasantness. Mila had a half-sister who mom took with her when she left. Mila had been very close to her little half-sister and was very protective of her. It was only natural for Mila to wonder whether she would be rejected when this baby arrived. I could try to give lip service to my intentions but she likely would not believe anything until she saw it in action. I was going to face some serious challenges carrying this baby and helping her adjust.

On December 29, I went to work at the church like any other day. I had talked the board into completing the terms of the severance package with the senior pastor before December 31, so both sides could put the situation behind them and move forward with clean slates in the new year. The pastor came in and I was able to give him his final check. I wrapped up my day and stopped by home before going into my evening job. I had a premonition that something wasn't right with the baby and had called the doctor's office late in the afternoon. The nurse calmed me down, but also gave me the straight scoop on what to do if anything changed.

The year 2000 had been very challenging with the vast amount of change and loss. I pretty much told God that afternoon that if I was going to lose this baby He better take care of it before the year ended. I did not want to start off the new year losing a baby.

At my second job I ate pizza for dinner and planned to work until around midnight as usual. By 9:00, I knew something was really wrong. I called my doctor and was told to head immediately to the hospital. In the most non alarming voice I could muster I called my mother and asked her to go to my house to watch the children because I needed my husband for something.

There in the triage area, I was told that the baby no longer had a heartbeat and I was miscarrying. I was overwhelmed. While I had struggled with the idea of bringing a baby into the mix at no point did I wish the baby would die. The medical team told me I could go home to finish miscarrying. I knew I couldn't emotionally handle that. The best option for me was going to be to stay in the hospital and have a D&E that night. They started asking me whether I wanted the baby saved for a Share burial which is a common burial of infants lost to miscarriage, stillbirth, or early infant death. I honestly couldn't make any decisions at that point. I was in shock and couldn't think clearly. I would have to depend on others to make those decisions. The nurses wisely advised that they would go ahead and hold my child. I could decide later if I wanted to go to the group funeral.

My mother's excitement for this grandchild would be short-lived. I had to call her to tell her that she would have to wait until heaven to meet the grandchild I had just told her she was supposed to meet next year and I would need her to stay there with the other two children for the night. She had just lost her mother in November and later admitted that losing this grandchild was so much harder to accept. Her mother had lived a full life but this baby never had a chance.

As I laid there trying to process the news and waiting for them to have the operating room available for me, we switched on the TV for some diversion. By divine channel surfing we landed on a series of Christian music videos. Phil Joel's video set to his song, "God is Watching Over You" came on. The song was on his album *Watching Over You* which had just released that year. I was familiar with the song because it was playing on the radio fairly often. I could not have asked for a more perfect song at that moment. The words replayed in my head throughout that long night and over the following weeks.

A second video came on which my husband was going to switch away from. It was the DC Talk song "My Friend" (So Long). The video opens with an ambulance and a patient being brought into the emergency room. The patient doesn't make it and the medical team goes out in the street dancing around with big plumes of feathers in a fanfare of saying so long. I tend to be very uneasy around medical facilities and the stress level definitely increases if I'm the patient. I don't know exactly what it was, but something in that video broke the tension I was feeling about being in the hospital.

> I TEND TO BE VERY UNEASY AROUND MEDICAL FACILITIES AND THE STRESS LEVEL DEFINITELY INCREASES IF I'M THE PATIENT

In the wee hours of December 30, I was taken into the operating room. Because I had eaten the pizza earlier in the evening it was deemed unsafe to put me fully under anesthesia. I would have to be completely awake and alert for everything that was happening. Because of the years of listening to Dr. John Willke talk about abortion procedures I knew what was going to happen. I am forever grateful for the team of nurses in that operating room that night. I told them that their most important job was to keep me distracted. We could talk about whatever random topics they came up with. As long as I could stay intellectually distracted things would be fine. If I got quiet and started to dwell on what was happening things would not go well. I don't remember what we talked about, but whatever random stuff it was got me through.

While I was in the recovery room, the nurse kept checking in with me to see if I needed pain meds. For whatever reason, I wasn't in pain—at least not physical pain. I did still have a glimmer of my sense of humor. When she informed me simply for future reference that my blood type was A positive I responded that I always did like A+'s in school. I couldn't change the situation, but I didn't have to be completely miserable through it.

The sun was coming up as I was leaving the hospital with an empty womb and empty arms. I returned home physically exhausted and still somewhat in shock. Part of me wanted to run and hide, but there was one thing I couldn't run from. There were two children in my home who needed me, and so I pushed my grief to the side to be the mom I needed to be for them.

I remember going to church the next day. I hadn't started spreading the word that I was pregnant so no one needed to know what had happened. I didn't really want to be around many people so rather than going into the main sanctuary I sat out in the overflow area of the lobby. That also meant it would be easy to escape to the ladies room to cry if I needed to. I was wrestling with so many different emotions. It may sound terrible but there was a part of me that was relieved. I had felt very overwhelmed with the thought of bringing a baby into this family. This family of four hadn't yet stabilized and I had now realized the massive trigger that a new baby would be for Mila. There was also the portion of me that was angry. As I sat there in the lobby a young woman came out from the main sanctuary. In the arms of this unwed teenager was a newborn. "God, it's not fair! I've done everything right. I waited for marriage. I'm financially stable enough to support a child. Why did I lose my baby and she has hers?" He had no answers for me that day and to be honest I'm not sure my heart would have been able to receive them anyway. I was angry. I was hurting. He could handle me venting and would still love me. He would use it all for good later I just couldn't see that far out.

THERE WERE TWO
CHILDREN IN MY HOME
WHO NEEDED ME, AND SO
I PUSHED MY GRIEF TO
THE SIDE TO BE THE MOM
I NEEDED TO BE FOR THEM

Chapter 6
Warrior Spirit Rise Up

O ver the next several months things began rapidly deteriorating in the home. Navo's natural temperament and defense mechanisms were easy to deal with. He was pretty good at listening to direction and tended not to challenge our authority. He would resort to humor to deescalate a situation or would simply retreat to a quiet corner. He was the peaceful child who easily fit into the routine. His heart was changing and it was reflected in his art. The deadly sword and blood drawings gave way to exquisite drawings of flowers complete with details and shading beyond the skill of a typical 9-year-old.

Mila on the other hand was much more of a handful. She had been the protector for her younger brother. With a strong-willed temperament she had challenged authority much more directly resulting in her receiving a disproportionate amount of the neglect and abuse. She had only lived a short life thus far but was very much damaged. Our home became a place of much chaos as she acted out. I didn't understand it. We were loving her and providing for her yet her behavior and reactions were out of control. It just didn't make any sense to me.

I remember seeking the help of a neighbor who worked at Children and Youth. He was formally trained in social work and surely could give wise counsel. The first thing he said was that this was a good sign. A good sign!? Was he crazy!? Where in the world did he get his education and what did they teach him? How in the world could this much chaos and friction in a home be a good sign? He told me that this demonstrated she felt safe and trusted us to let everything inside come out. I was not liking his explanation. Great, she trusts me and now is making my life a living hell... and this is a good thing!?

> HOW IN THE WORLD COULD THIS MUCH CHAOS AND FRICTION IN A HOME BE A GOOD SIGN?

He helped point us in the right direction to begin navigating the world of social services and counseling for these types of issues. We landed in the offices of a well-respected secular counseling agency. The woman talked to Mila and then talked to us. Her words were even less encouraging. She said things would probably get worse before they got better. Are you kidding me? I don't think I can handle anything worse. Unfortunately she was correct. Things did get worse.

I learned the pattern. Things get out of control, call crisis intervention, go to the hospital emergency room, get a referral, head to the children's inpatient facility, child is admitted, a few days later child is released, and a few days later the pattern repeats. It was a cycle I did not want to be stuck in, but nothing was working and I was way outside of my area of expertise. I remember calling crisis intervention one day and the woman on the other end of the phone casually said, "Oh yes, I am familiar with your case. We discussed it today in the staff meeting." Wonderful, we are such regulars for the crisis intervention team that they recognize me when I call. I wouldn't mind being on a first name basis with any of the people on the team, but definitely did not want it to be because of calling so frequently, especially given the nature and place of their employment. Sadly I was becoming so well known in these circles that while sitting in the emergency room I could often call directly to the inpatient facility and skip the referral of the hospital. The ER receptionist would look puzzled when I would ask her to take our name off the list because we were already being accepted at the inpatient facility. Depending on who was working the desk that day they might interject, "that's impossible. You have to be referred." Well ma'am, we're kind of like regulars up there. Once again, not the type of place you want to be a regular.

It seemed to be a never-ending cycle and things weren't getting any better. If anything they seemed to be getting worse. Maybe it wasn't actually getting worse, but rather we were becoming so fatigued with no hope or end in sight that we were waning in our ability to cope. I remember one day when things had been particularly exhausting and the doctor would not admit Mila for the weekend that I actually resorted to asking them to admit me. Their response was something like "we can't admit you because we don't deem you to be a risk to yourself." I responded with "what if I tell you I want to harm myself?" They weren't buying it. "What if I cut myself? And is a paper cut sufficient? I really don't like the sight of blood." Obviously they realized they were dealing with someone who was rational but on the verge of becoming irrational in her desperation. It was probably wise that they admitted Mila for that weekend otherwise they might have been looking for rooms for three patients and temporary foster parents for one.

Sometimes they would prescribe medications in an attempt to keep Mila under control. I remember one time bringing her home and while I didn't like the child in her normal state I liked the child in this state even less. She sat there at the dining room table staring off into space. I would call her name and there was quite a delay before I'd get a drawn-out glassy-eyed "wha-a-a-at?" While I didn't like chaotic Mila, I really didn't like drugged Mila who didn't even seem to be there. I reached out to another friend of mine who worked in social work and had more training than I did. She was adamant that I needed to take her off that stuff.

THERE WAS NO WAY I WANTED MY CHILD DRUGGED ALL THE TIME

It was apparently the same type of drug they would use on an adult who showed up in the ER combative and strung out on illegal drugs. There was no way I wanted my child drugged all of the time. The medications seemed to be an attempt at a Band-Aid on the problem and I felt this was a set of problems that could and must be fixed without medications. She did not have a chemical imbalance. She had behavior problems stemming from abuse.

We were desperate for any help we could get and once in a church service she started acting up. We got the attention of an usher and the pastor sent a very kind couple out to the lobby with us to help give us wise counsel. They became a lifeline I could call any time for advice and suggestions.

One particular Sunday we took Mila forward for prayer. A couple prayed for God to intervene in the situation and then the husband spoke directly to me. He reiterated the words I had heard so many times in church but somehow had never made it from my head to deep in my heart. The Bible says, "Greater is he that is in you, than he that is in the world" (I John 4:4b KJV), and "these signs will accompany those who believe: In my name they will drive out demons; they will speak in new tongues; they will pick up snakes with their hands; and when they drink deadly poison, it will not hurt them at all; they will place their hands on sick people, and they will get well" (Mark 16:17-18 NIV). You have authority in Jesus Name over whatever is plaguing this child.

It was definitely one of those God moments because there was a pattern to it. When God wants to deliver a very direct and important message to me via a person He always uses a tall man, presumably because I subconsciously associate them with authority. He also always uses someone I don't know because He wants to bypass my head and relational filters and get the message to my heart. He never lets me remember anything else about the person that would allow me to recognize the individual because He doesn't want me to associate the message with the individual. Some might suggest those men are actually angels and it is possible they are; however I prefer to believe they are actual humans who are obeying God when He tells them to do something. That Sunday morning those words sank deep into my heart in a way they never had before. I did have authority over whatever this was and it was time to exercise my authority.

I had authority and at times would exercise it and see results but then it was like there was still an open door and things would quickly return to the dysfunctional status quo. It still felt like I was being defeated on all fronts. I almost dreaded coming home from work each day because I knew what I was likely walking into. At one point we had wrap-around services so on those days I would come home to a counselor hanging out in my house for hours. Mila would be fine while the counselor was there but then things would start up again when she left.

Fortunately during this season I was still working at the church. The church gave me considerable flexibility to deal with the crazy schedule of appointments and day programs that required long daily drives. With the shifts that were happening at the church and the sense that I had accomplished the primary mission for which I had originally been brought on full time I was feeling like it was time to return to the corporate world. I would not have the same flexibility once I switched employers. The madness needed to end.

During those challenging days God gave me a mental picture of a woman standing in the gap of a stone wall with arms lifted up and looking out to beautiful green grass and trees ahead of her. The image originated from two scriptures. The first is Ezekiel 22:30a "I looked for someone among them who would build up the wall and stand before me in the gap on behalf of the land." The second is Isaiah 6:8 "Then I heard the voice of the Lord saying, 'Whom shall I send? And who will go for us?' And I said, 'Here am I. Send me.'" I had been called to stand in the gap on my daughter's behalf and a brighter future had to be out there ahead of us. I just couldn't see it yet.

I loved Mila but none of us could handle any more of the chaos. She didn't seem to be responding to anything anyone was trying. I surely didn't have the answers. She was fine in the classroom, but at home she was a disaster. In an institution she seemed to be perfectly functional but once home the problems came out again. If the wrap around person was in the house things were fine but when she left it felt as if all progress was lost.

ONE DAY, MY HUSBAND HAD REACHED HIS BREAKING POINT AND TASKED ME WITH GETTING RID OF HER

One day, my husband had reached his breaking point and tasked me with getting rid of her. The plan was that I would take her to the inpatient facility and we would never go back. Children and Youth would have to find another family for her.

She was being particularly challenging that morning and thus began the normal routine of heading to the ER. I was almost as much of a mess as she was because I knew what I was supposed to be doing. We got the referral and headed to the inpatient facility. In the car, she was yelling and carrying on. She was threatening to roll down the windows and yell things to the other drivers in neighboring cars at the traffic light. Why does the light have to be red? This is just too much drama. I don't want other people to see or hear her rants. They don't have all of the background and I don't want them making judgment calls based on the outbursts of a very vocal ten-year-old. Please light just turn green.

The closer I got to the inpatient facility the harder it was becoming. She knew where we were headed and didn't want to go. I knew this might be the last time I would see her and didn't really want to go there either. I desperately wanted a fix to this situation but had run out of options, ideas, connections, and the energy to keep fighting.

With just a few miles left in the drive I clearly heard God say "Are you sure this is my will?" I was already having a hard time with this and now was completely wrecked. I knew in my heart I was not to abandon her, but there was nothing left of me. I flashed to the memory of sitting there when she prayed to accept Jesus into her heart. I told her He would always love her and never abandon her. I told her how we are to be like Jesus. If Jesus never gave up on me how could I give up on her? Was I just a hypocrite? She was just a ten-year-old child. She didn't ask for any of the crap that she went through. So many adults had failed her and here I was being the next one in the line. "God, I know it's not your will, but I don't know what to do anymore."

I don't remember how I made it through the check-in process and answering the staff's questions. I don't even remembering saying goodbye to her. I was just trying to get through what I had to do before the torrent of tears started.

I can't tell you how I saw to drive home that day. The tears just wouldn't stop. I knew I was to be her mom, but I had nothing left in me to give. I had tried everything I could think of and I was physically, emotionally, and spiritually exhausted. It had been months and months of chaos in our home and I had reached the end of my own rope. I've heard it said so many times that "faith isn't faith until it's all you are holding on to" and at that point I wasn't even sure I had any faith left. Hebrews 11:1 in the Passion Translation says this:

> "Now faith brings our hopes into reality and becomes the foundation needed to acquire the things we long for. It is all the evidence required to prove what is still unseen."

I had lost my foundation through all of the fighting and fatigue and thus my hopes were not becoming reality. Faith needed to rise up again.

For a week we did not call her or visit her. It was exactly the break that I needed. I was able to regain enough of my strength to consider giving this one more shot. I drove by myself to the inpatient facility to visit her. By now the staff knew where we were at in dealing with her and the issues. They were trying to make it abundantly clear to her that she had run out of chances. They could not make any promises to her that her family would come back but if they did she needed to understand that things were going to have to change. She was going to have to cooperate or she may never see her brother or any of her natural extended family ever again.

As I walked into the hospital this time it was as if God removed the blinders from my eyes. As I sat there in her room I watched across the hallway as a nurse went into the room of a young boy who was acting up. She gave him a cocktail of pills to calm him down. I suddenly saw him through new eyes. He was crying out for attention and no amount of pills was going to fix that. He needed a family who would love him and help him heal from whatever trauma he had gone through in his young life. It was clear to me that Mila needed a family to help her heal and become functional. No institution was going to be able to fix her.

My heart knew we were the family for her, but I still didn't understand the root of all of the chaos. To date no one had been able to give me a clear answer on what was going on inside of her. I thought back to a few things I learned from the psychology classes I took in college and some things I had heard about techniques for counseling children. I remembered something about counselors using play therapy. I didn't really know the "how to" details but was pretty sure it was something about the counselor distracting the child while playing games with them. Sometimes the child would open up and talk about what was going on inside. At this point I was not a trained counselor and none of the trained counselors had been able to give me anything to work with. What did I have to lose by trying?

THE FIRST KEY PIECE TO THE PUZZLE WAS THAT SHE SAW LOVE AS WATER IN A GLASS RATHER THAN WATER IN A FAUCET...

Mila and I went to the common room where the toys were kept and started to play. I asked her if she knew why she acted up at various times. She started talking and I began understanding what was behind her actions. The first key piece to the puzzle was that she saw love as water in a glass rather than water in a faucet. There was a finite amount of love available and she had to compete for it. I could not possibly love her, and her brother, and my husband simultaneously. Monopolizing the attention was her way of attempting to guarantee that she would get the love or what she thought was love. I could see this was a messed up way of viewing the world but it was the world that was real to her.

The second key piece to the puzzle was the messed up cause and effect construct in her mind. In her short life, she had observed too many instances of men showing affection to a woman followed by them abusing the woman. In her mind, there was a cause and effect pattern. She believed if you prevent affection you prevent abuse. While in some instances this would be correct, not every male and female relationship follows this pattern. Not every male showing affection to a woman would then abuse the woman. She had emotionally attached to me, and now I understood why she would suddenly act up if my husband came near me to show me any affection. While she had no observations to substantiate her beliefs, she believed he was going to abuse me so if she interrupted the affection she could prevent the abuse. She was trying to protect me. It was another completely messed up way of viewing the world but it made sense given what she had observed in her short lifetime.

Equipped with this divine insight, I went home with a mission. I had two very specific issues that a counselor would have to tackle and I knew that she was not going to get the help she needed where she was. She needed to come home where the peer pressure would be to become a healthy functioning member of society and she needed good Christian counselors who could help guide us in breaking the stronghold of messed up thinking. It was my responsibility to find counselors to help her. A faith-filled warrior spirit like I had never experienced in my lifetime was rising up. God's will was that I parent this child. I was going to find help for her and nothing was going to get in my way.

> *Finally, be strong in the Lord and in his mighty power. Put on the full armor of God, so that you can take your stand against the devil's schemes. For our struggle is not against flesh and blood, but against the rulers, against the authorities, against the powers of this dark world and against the spiritual forces of evil in the heavenly realms. Therefore put on the full armor of God, so that when the day of evil comes, you may be able to stand your ground, and after you have done everything, to stand. Stand firm then, with the belt of truth buckled around your waist, with the breastplate of righteousness in place, and with your feet fitted with the readiness that comes from the gospel of peace. In addition to all this, take up the shield of faith, with which you can extinguish all the flaming arrows of the evil one. Take the helmet of salvation and the sword of the Spirit, which is the word of God.*
>
> EPHESIANS 6:10-17 NIV

My battle was not against the child but against the lies that the child was led to believe. My feet were firmly planted and my heels were digging in. I was going to stand for her no matter what. She was being tormented in her mind and I wasn't going to tolerate it anymore. "For God hath not given us the spirit of fear; but of power, and of love, and of a sound mind" (2 Timothy 1:7 KJV). She needed and deserved a sound mind.

I remember hearing many sermons on the faith of the Canaanite woman and I was identifying with her.

> *Leaving that place, Jesus withdrew to the region of Tyre and Sidon. A Canaanite woman from that vicinity came to him, crying out, "Lord, Son of David, have mercy on me! My daughter is demon-possessed and suffering terribly." Jesus did not answer a word. So his disciples came to him and urged him, "Send her away, for she keeps crying out after us." He answered, "I was sent only to the lost sheep of Israel." The woman came and knelt before him. "Lord, help me!" she said. He replied, "It is not right to take the children's bread and toss it to the dogs." "Yes it is, Lord," she said. "Even the dogs eat the crumbs that fall from their master's table." Then Jesus said to her, "Woman, you have great faith! Your request is granted." And her daughter was healed at that moment.*
>
> MATTHEW 15:21-28, NIV

The Canaanite woman knew Jesus could heal her daughter and was not taking "no" for an answer. Her tenacity, persistence, and faith paid off and her daughter was healed. I got the same fire in my belly that the Canaanite woman had. Hebrews 13:8 says, "Jesus Christ is the same yesterday and today and forever."

"Jesus," I prayed, "you did it back then and you can do it today. You healed her daughter and you can heal mine. I'm not taking 'no' for an answer!"

I sat down with the phone book and started calling every Christian counseling agency in Lancaster and York County. There had to be someone who could help us and I was going to find that person. With each call I would explain the situation and ask whether they could handle our case. I heard lots of "no, we don't handle that type of case." I didn't care. I was determined and just moved to the next agency on the list and dialed the number. With one call I reached a pastor who had adopted children and his advice was to turn her back to Children and Youth because she would cost me everything. I politely thanked him for his counsel, hung up the phone and said "no thanks, that's not what God told me to do."

Eventually I got a woman on the phone who said "yes, we can help you." Finally, someone says they can help! I asked for an appointment to which she responded that she would put us on the waiting list. "Oh no, maybe you didn't understand, I need to schedule an appointment." She came back with the same waiting list answer and I responded back clarifying that perhaps she was misunderstanding me. "I need to schedule an appointment." I think she was getting the message that I was desperate and probably realized she was going to have to offer me something to get me off the phone. She offered the next best option she could come up with which was that over the upcoming weekend they were doing a training program for lay counselors. I was welcome to attend the training during which I might pick up a few ideas of things to try. In the meantime, if they had a cancelation she would try to get us in. I finally had a glimmer of hope.

The morning of the training program came, and I was there at the front of the registration line. "I was the one who spoke to you on the phone and needs an appointment for her daughter." If it wasn't clear on the phone that I was serious and desperate, they were getting the message now. I was the mom who was going to be relentless and harrass them until they got her daughter in for counseling. I don't know if they had cancellations and we made it to the top of the waiting list, or if the staff looked at each other and decided someone should take on some overtime to deal with us, but within a week or two they were able to squeeze us in. That team of prayer warrior counselors did in just a few weeks what the secular inpatient facility couldn't accomplish in months.

THE CHAOS STOPPED AND THE HEALING BEGAN

Jesus, You really are the same yesterday, today and forever and You showed up to replace the lies with truth. The chaos stopped and healing began.

What differentiated this counseling team from others was the approach they took. While they had formal training in psychology and counseling, they also incorporated a prayer ministry approach.

When Jesus performed the miracle of turning the water into wine, he changed the essence of the liquid. Why was he able to do that? He was given authority by God, the Creator of the water, to change it. Only the Creator can truly change the created.

If you were holding a lemon and wanted an orange, you could try to paint it orange. When the fruit is hit with rain or rough times, the true nature of the lemon is revealed. You could work really hard and use a die to make the orange color go deeper. When you squeeze it, lemon juice, not orange juice, will come out. Even if you change the color, add flavoring and sugar, the reality is that at its most basic essence, you still have lemon juice. Often secular counseling attempts to teach a person how to make better life choices. It gets to the head and perhaps a little deeper. Very often, when tough times come, the individual reverts back to their old ways. The "counseling" that we found which made revolutionary changes in Mila was less about putting constructive ideas and strategies in her head and more about helping her hear the voice of her Creator, who could change her from the inside out.

Why was I able to fight to find a solution for her? It was because my Creator spoke directly into my heart. It didn't matter what a well-meaning pastor said on the phone; I knew without a doubt what I was to do. Why will I explain later that I had peace when I lost my second baby? I had peace because my Creator showed me where she was. If the wounded person is told by their Creator, the very one who knit them together in their mother's womb, that they are loved and valued, it changes him or her in a way that not even the most educated experienced counselor could ever do.

Chapter 7
Flip the Goal

I started in a Montessori program when I was just a toddler. When it was time for first grade I transitioned into a public school and stayed there through second grade. I then moved to a private Christian school for third through sixth grade. When it came time for middle school I was moved to the public school where I remained through graduation. It was discovered in my files that I had tested as gifted and because the public school had multiple tracks I was put with the students in the more challenging classes. I worked hard and did well. In my family As were great, Bs were ok, and Cs would have generated some less than optimal conversations unless they were in art or handwriting.

In God's infinite wisdom or endless humor He gave the academically oriented person two children who were not.

Mila and Navo arrived in late September. We were advised not to move them from their existing public school because of wanting to maintain friendships and stability in their schooling. It would end up being the first school year that Navo remained with one teacher in one school for an entire year. Mila was out quite a bit in the second half of the year as we worked through her counseling issues so fourth grade in the Christian school would be her first full year for stable education.

Within a week or two of having the children, I was realizing that Mila could not read. Age-wise, she belonged in fourth grade but was sitting in third with Navo. I was not a trained educator but knew something wasn't right. I distinctly remember being in the public school and being able to read. I can't remember whether it was first or second grade but I remember the teacher giving us a challenge. For every book we read, we could get a paper link to put in the chain and if as a class we could get the chain all of the way around the room, out the door, down the hall, and to the principal's office we would get a pizza party. Even at age 6 and 7, I was goal-oriented. I figured out that the skinnier the book the more I could read and the faster we could get our party. The teacher changed the rules for me and I had to read chapter books. I wasn't particularly happy about that but we did eventually get our party. I realized that Mila was at an age where she should be able to read, but couldn't. I headed in to meet her teacher.

Her teacher was a very kind woman who was closing in on retirement, and apparently, I was the first parent to show up in her classroom in years. She shared with me the stark realities that I, who grew up in a rather functional suburban home, couldn't even begin to fathom. She agreed with me that Mila should be able to read. She then clued me in that Mila and Navo had likely missed many of the critical basics because of being moved around so much and likely not even being in any school for extended periods. Moving between states and school districts likely meant they completely missed topics which were not always taught in the same sequences at different places. She then explained to me how she was barely able to teach because much of her day was consumed with addressing social problems. She had children who would leave school at the end of the day and not see another responsible adult until they came back to school the next morning. They may go home to a single parent home and mom may be working second shift somewhere or could be inebriated or strung out on drugs. Maybe grandma was in the picture desperately trying to do whatever she could do because both parents were in jail. At times, this teacher would need to send a child to the cafeteria to get breakfast because they hadn't eaten anything since lunch the day before. She may have to send a child to the nurse because she saw bruises or wounds that suggested abuse. She told me she had 25 children in her classroom and 23 needed new homes. The two who didn't need new homes were the two I now had. In my naivety, I thought these were big city problems, but was learning they were right here in my small city.

I THOUGHT THESE WERE BIG CITY PROBLEMS, BUT WAS LEARNING THEY WERE RIGHT HERE

When the first quarter's report card arrived, it was very discouraging for an academically oriented mom. Across the board was the feedback of failure. I don't have a background in teaching and definitely did not feel equipped to handle two children who were so far behind, especially in a school where the teacher struggled to get to do what she was trained to and really wanted to do. I talked to the principal of the school about my concern with their inability to read and was met with what came across as a cavalier attitude that many children were struggling, but mine would probably catch up on their own. It felt as if she had given up because the problem was too great. She seemed more concerned about whether the children walked on the grass versus sidewalk than whether they could actually read. We would get through the end of the school year but I was definitely looking for a different school that would have teachers who could focus on teaching and would have the resources to address the gaps or learning disabilities or whatever was going on with these two.

While we struggled through that year in the public school I didn't really know what to do to help with homework but opted to go back to some of my Montessori days for ideas. Perhaps when it came to math I could try the tactile hands-on learning and use pens on the table to explain addition and subtraction. Even using cookies in the example didn't seem to connect. It felt hopeless. Mila and Navo really didn't think they were capable of getting anything better than Fs. It was becoming apparent that I would have to reprogram their failure mentality into "I can" or at least "I'll try." While that's a great idea how in the world do I do that?

> I WOULD HAVE TO REPROGRAM THEIR FAILURE MENTALITY INTO "I CAN" OR AT LEAST "I'LL TRY"

Often after school I would have to pick the children up and bring them back to the church office with me. We lived in a different district than the school they were attending and thus we couldn't get bussing for them to the house. They were also too young and too volatile with each other to be left alone as latch key children. One day they were with me and we were walking down a long straight hallway in the church when Navo suddenly started doing cartwheels down the hallway. The light bulb lit up in my head. The goal needed to flip, literally. I needed to find something where the children could be successful which would reorient their thinking and self-esteem. We could work on the academics later. The cartwheels suggested I should try gymnastics.

I enrolled the two of them in gymnastics and they excelled. These were athletically and artistically gifted children, a far cry from their academically and musically gifted new mother. With the success in gymnastics their mindset began to shift. They now understood what excellence was, and if you try something enough times there's a good chance you will get it and succeed. That mindset shift began translating to their academics. When the next report card arrived I called my mother and with great excitement reported that the children got Ds.

She paused, "Is this Cathie? Did you say Ds?" She was naturally struggling to understand how the child she remembered who would be traumatized by anything less than an A in high school could now be the adult who sounded so happy with Ds. Had I completely lost my mind? It started to make sense when I added that last quarter we had all Fs. Now she understood. My excitement wasn't the Ds. My excitement was progress in a positive direction. They may not be destined for Harvard but they were not going to fail and drop out.

At the end of that first school year the decision was made that the following year Mila and Navo would be moving to a private

Christian school. This new school was known to be the best in the county for children like ours. It had a long reputation for excellence in specialized educational resources and could handle significant learning gaps and learning disabilities. They would also reinforce the values we were teaching at home. It was wonderful to partner with educators who were so well equipped to do what I couldn't do. I didn't always immediately understand some of the seemingly foreign and disconnected techniques they used in the learning disability side, but there was science behind it that did make some sense. I guess it worked because both of them graduated with their classes and are succeeding as adults.

"Where there is no vision the people perish"

PROVERBS 29:18

"Where there is no vision the teenager may fail and drop out of school."

CATHIE

I remember a period in middle school when they were struggling with why they needed to do all this boring stuff in the classroom. They couldn't imagine going to college for anything. They had no concept that any job could be even remotely enjoyable for them. The "think outside the box" mom had to get creative to drive home the point that no matter what, they should at least get a high school diploma. I took them to an open house for an art school. The people at the registration desk thought I was a little crazy bringing middle schoolers in for a visit but there was a method to my madness. I wanted them to see that there are programs after high school that would be in things that interested them at that time – i.e. fashion, graphic arts, etc. The open house included information on job placement so they were able to hear about the types of jobs that graduates were getting. Naturally, the school was probably presenting only the few very elite, very cool and exciting job opportunities that their graduates were pursuing. That was just fine with me because even if a bit of it was a little inflated in the reality, it was getting to my end goal of casting a vision for the future. I needed Mila and Navo to make the connection that to get those cool jobs requires a post-high school program and to get in you must have the high school diploma. "Suffering" through the boring stuff was just a necessary stepping stone to greater things.

Good parenting, at times, requires creativity. It isn't necessarily about being an expert in everything yourself. A willingness to look for others who are talented at what they do and can positively influence your child can demonstrate great wisdom. Middle schoolers often discount what their parents know but amazingly enough may listen to another adult. In the case of the art school I made that reality work for me.

GOOD PARENTING,
AT TIMES, REQUIRES
CREATIVITY—
NOT NECESSARILY
BEING AN EXPERT IN
EVERYTHING YOURSELF

Chapter 8
Choosing to Adopt

When Mila and Navo's biological mom walked out of their lives, there was no legal closure. She simply dropped them and some of their info off with her mother and left town. When Children and Youth became involved, they were pulling the children from the care of their grandmother but she didn't have any legal rights to them either, so Children and Youth wasn't compelled to do anything about legal rights. The children were placed with us under a loose definition of kinship care but with no legal rights. Technically, we didn't have the right to get them medical coverage through the state. Technically, we didn't have the right to enroll them in school. Technically, we didn't have the right to do anything. In practice, if a strong mother-type figure is standing in front of someone advocating for a child whom she obviously considers as her own, there's a good chance legal rights will not even come up. This mom would not relent, so legal rights or not, I was going to make things happen. Most people know not to mess with a momma bear with cubs in the wild. I was a momma bear and would likely have growled at you if you messed with my cubs or didn't let me get what I needed for my cubs.

There came a point when I realized that I had bonded so much with these children that I wanted the legal rights so no one could take them from me. It was a little bit selfish, but I no longer wanted the uncertainty about "what if biological mom comes back one day." I had survived a miscarriage but had never bonded with that child like I had bonded with these two. I would be completely devastated if someone took these children away from me. We had bought a bigger house to more easily accommodate the family of four. Our finances were set up around making sure we could afford their Christian school. These children were very much a part of my life and I wanted it to remain that way.

I called the attorney I had spoken to before getting married and said we wanted to start the process. To finalize an adoption, both parents' rights would have to be terminated. For dad, the only option was to publish a legal notice in New York City which was the last known whereabouts for him.

When it came to mom, we had a possible address. This was my husband's niece, and I wasn't sure how she might react to getting a bunch of legal documents. Would it seem harsh and insensitive? Would she panic thinking that she was in trouble with the law? Our attorney was open to us sending a cover letter explaining our heart in choosing to start this legal process. As much as I could, I attempted to put myself in her shoes. I was asking her to officially give up her rights to the children she had carried and had parented for years. Would this feel like a relief or would she suddenly want to come back into their lives? I couldn't judge her for walking out. She was forced by someone else into parenting at the age of 13. A hospital in New York helped her deliver the baby and knew her age. Fifteen months later, she returned to deliver another child. The state of New York gave out birth certificates for the children with her age and the significantly greater age of the father and apparently did nothing to help this young mother. From age 13 to 22, she did the best she could. I didn't have to start parenting until 27. I had all of my teenage years free to do what I wanted and was supported and protected by my parents. She didn't have any of that. I shared with her the great things that were happening for Mila and Navo and my hope that she would be open to legally releasing them. We wanted to guarantee them stability and afford them all of the benefits of being our legal children. I was open to her coming back into their lives on some level in the future if she wanted.

I'll never forget the day the attorney called to tell me that in all his years of practice he had never had this happen, and for the record, he had considerable experience. He had gotten a call from their biological mom and she was not going to contest the adoption. She would sign anything we needed. As long as dad didn't show up and contest, it would be smooth sailing. On September 11, 2003, in the Lancaster County Court House, Mila and Navo Guzman officially became Rosados.

I don't know if it was that I became more aware of adoptive families after adopting or if there's something about us that we attract each other, but I have come to know what seems to be a disproportionate number of families touched by adoption. Some families had no problems having natural children but reached a point where they decided they still had more love to give and rather than add another natural child chose to adopt. Some couples knew going into marriage that natural children would not be an option and chose adoption to create their family. Some couples struggled seemingly endlessly with infertility and chose to adopt. Some because of death or unfortunate circumstances in a family sudden took in and adopted the children of a friend or relative.

Adoptive families are in all walks of life. They come in all shapes and sizes. There are adopted sibling groups, various children who are now through adoption part of sibling groups, or adopted only children. There are combinations of adopted and natural children in the same family. Some families are all one shade, extremes of dark and light, or a combination of every shade of the rainbow. Each one is unique and beautiful.

We've had fun with our rainbow family over the years. I remember once going to a Japanese hibachi restaurant, which interestingly was being run by a Chinese family. We had an eclectic combination of my mother, brother, husband, stepdaughter, step-granddaughter, adopted children, a Taiwanese exchange student, and a Korean exchange student. Our waiter gave up trying to figure out the family tree sitting before him. I remember when we moved into our new house and Mila came to get me because the neighbors wanted to meet me. As Mila said on the way down to their house, "This is going to be fun." The woman looked at me, looked at her, and likely thought something like, "Maybe she's the husband's daughter?" I bet her preconceived notion given Mila's dark skin, dark eyes, and dark curly hair didn't quite match my fair skin, blue eyes, and light hair. Yes, Mila looks incredible in a white dress and I look like a ghost. God gave her an incredible built-in tan and I apparently missed the pigment line. Any efforts to change my shade with sun-worshipping does not go well, so I've resigned myself to accepting that white dresses will never be a regular part of my wardrobe. My natural children came along and it took a while before they ever consciously noticed that their siblings looked different. Family and love are color blind.

FAMILY AND
LOVE ARE
COLOR BLIND

Chapter 9
A Glimpse of Heaven

A fter finalizing the adoption, I almost expected to get pregnant immediately. I knew of countless stories where couples had struggled with infertility for years, chose to adopt, and then suddenly conceived a natural child. I would often hear people say that the stress was off and that's why they were finally successful. My theory was that God had a specific child already picked out whom He wanted them to adopt and once they were obedient and the timing was right, He would give them the natural child they also desired.

> *Trust in the Lord, and do good; dwell in the land and befriend faithfulness. Delight yourself in the Lord, and he will give you the desires of your heart. Commit your way to the Lord; trust in him, and he will act. He will bring forth your righteousness as the light, and your justice as the noonday.*
>
> PSALM 37:3-6 ESV

You will again obey the Lord and follow all his commands
I am giving you today. Then the Lord your God will make
you most prosperous in all the work of your hands and
in the fruit of your womb, the young of your livestock
and the crops of your land. The Lord will again delight
in you and make you prosperous, just as he delighted in
your ancestors, if you obey the Lord your God and keep
his commands and decrees that are written in this Book
of the Law and turn to the Lord your God with all your
heart and with all your soul.

DEUTERONOMY 30: 8-10

"Okay, God, I have officially adopted Mila and Navo. Are you going to give me a natural child now?" Month after month, the answer was no. I had not been on birth control and still had not conceived again after losing that first baby almost four years earlier. It was becoming doubtful that I'd ever have a natural child.

In December 2004, right around the fourth anniversary of my first miscarriage, I learned I was finally pregnant again. I was excited but also nervous. I called the doctor and wanted to make sure I did everything right. I was not very far along and they did the blood tests to confirm I was pregnant. I definitely was, but subsequent blood tests weren't showing what they would expect. The hormone levels were not rising at a pace consistent with a viable pregnancy. I was sent for ultrasounds and they also weren't showing what they would expect. They expected a heartbeat but there was no heartbeat. The doctor was hesitant to say it wasn't a viable pregnancy but things were not looking good. As the days passed I was getting the sinking feeling that this baby was also not going to make it. The stress was definitely starting to get to me, and one Saturday morning while making waffles for the family (which at this point also included two exchange students from Taiwan and South Korea), I collapsed. I quickly regained consciousness but it was becoming apparent that we were going to have to tell the children what was going on.

I desperately needed whatever peace could be found in this situation. I wanted a clear answer. Was this child going to make it or was this one also going to go to heaven before I held him or her in my arms? As I was resting in bed one day God gave me the answer I needed in the form of a very clear vision. I saw my grandmother who had passed away in 2000 shortly before I lost my first child. To her right was standing a little boy around 4 years of age. In her left arm was a baby girl. That vision immediately confirmed for me that my child was in heaven and we could move forward with whatever the doctors needed to do here.

I told my mother what I saw. Her first question was what her mother looked like. I've never been one to be overly observant about fine details and in this case the details weren't as important as the message God was trying to speak directly into my heart. I didn't remember many details but what I could tell my mother was that the woman I saw I knew to be her mother. She was not the frail bent over woman we last saw on earth, but was standing up straight and had the muscle tone of a 30-year-old. She had the energy level and strength required to care for my two children. I didn't see details about my two children other than they were a boy and a girl and their ages and sizes were consistent with what they would have been here on earth. What I needed to come away with in my heart was that my baby was in heaven and in good hands. I believe God chose to use my maternal grandmother to relay that message because she was the closest relative I had in Heaven at the time and the one most closely associated with my spiritual identity and heritage of faith.

I knew when I went into the next doctor's appointment a few days later that it was just a matter of earthly formality at this point. We decided I could probably miscarry naturally when my body was ready. That would have been an acceptable plan except that my body didn't seem to want to let go.

I was at work one day and was in a great deal of pain and very, very dizzy. I was starting to pop over the counter pain killers like they were candy. I called the doctor's office and they really didn't like what they heard. They asked me to come in right away. I told the key people at the office that I needed to leave and there was a chance I may not be back for a few days. They didn't know anything about what was going on, and I didn't want to tell them. They were visibly concerned but given I wasn't saying anything they felt it best not to ask.

> I WAS STARTING TO POP OVER THE COUNTER PAIN KILLERS LIKE THEY WERE CANDY

At the doctor's office, they expressed their concern that I might be heading for infections and that the best plan would likely be another D&E. I agreed. The plan was that I would go in on February 11, Navo's birthday. I didn't like the date. This would mean having another child's birthday associated with a loss. My first D&E had been on my step daughter's birthday. Fortunately or unfortunately they couldn't get the operating room for the eleventh and had to reschedule. They gave me the option of the tenth or waiting until the following week. There was no way I could wait through the weekend. I was already popping pain killers every few hours and having a hard time holding everything together. On February 10, I went into the hospital for the D&E.

It was a little rough as they were prepping me with IVs and taking the requisite blood samples. I don't like seeing nurses and phlebotomists work, so I try to look the opposite direction. Unfortunately, I had one on each side so there was nowhere to look. The one with the IV was used to working in a different part of the hospital with different equipment. She was having a rough time getting the IV in, which also meant I was having a rough time. I did not want to stress her out and make it still more challenging, so I tried to be as patient of a patient as possible. Eventually, one of the other nurses realized this was likely quite miserable and painful for me and opted to take over. It was a welcome change.

This time around, I had the opportunity to plan so I didn't eat that morning and thus they could put me completely under anesthesia. I had a nice short nap and came to in the recovery room. In a little while I was ready to leave and once again I was pushed to the hospital doors in a wheelchair with an empty womb and empty arms.

The doctor did not give me much hope after that second loss. If I really wanted children, her recommendation was to start working with a fertility specialist. Given my strong pro-life convictions, I wrestled with the various options. If they gave me drugs to potentially increase the number of eggs, there was a chance I could conceive multiples. If it were deemed unsafe to try to carry all of them to term, that would mean they would likely advise me to selectively reduce. There was no way I could do that. I decided I shouldn't risk the drug option. If we ended up trying invitro, it was possible we would end up with multiple embryos. I would again struggle and feel responsible for trying to carry each and every one of them. What if we ended up with a dozen viable embryos? Was I willing to sign up to carry 6-12 pregnancies? I just didn't feel I could do that either. As a side note, several years later I learned of "snowflake babies." They are the "leftover" embryos from in-vitro that a family could opt to adopt out to a woman who couldn't conceive but could carry. She would end up carrying a baby that didn't share any of her genetic material but with whom she would bond through the pregnancy and then legally adopt after birth. That actually sounds like a very neat option, but I think I'm now past planning for any more children through childbirth.

Our insurance would not cover much of what the fertility specialists would recommend trying, and I just didn't have any peace about spending the money when they couldn't give me guarantees. I had two adopted children at home who needed extra resources for their education. There was more of a guarantee of return if I spent the money on Mila and Navo's education. I had to lay the desire for natural children at the feet of Jesus. If I were to have them, then He would have to figure out how to get it done and I was choosing acceptance.

Chapter 10
Can I Dream Again?

❧ ——————————————— ❧

I accepted the loss of my second baby pretty well and went on with life. I had the opportunity that summer to go to Taiwan on a business trip, which is something I would not have been able to do had I continued to carry my daughter. She had been due around the end of August. Even though I was no longer pregnant, I had not forgotten her due date. We decided to host my mother-in-law's birthday party at our house, and we planned the party for that weekend which was pretty close to her birthday. Surely, the busy-ness of the party would keep me distracted from dwelling on the date. Unbeknownst to me, there were two young, unmarried, pregnant women in the extended family that summer. Both gave birth in August, and they came to the party with brand new baby girls. I could not bring myself to be in the same room with them. The sight of the two babies had reopened the wounds. All of those feelings of "it's not fair" were right back up at the surface. I was much better off retreating to the kitchen and playing servant hostess. As a wounded animal would growl and bite if provoked, I knew my tongue would lash out if I were provoked. Avoiding confrontation proved to be the best way to keep my tongue under control.

A woman who has lost a child or children and still has deep wounds can be triggered by things she may not expect. It's ideal if she can recognize she's been triggered and not take it out on others. Sometimes, it is wise to simply avoid situations that are likely to be triggers if the wounds are too raw. Going to a baby shower right after my losses would not have been wise, just as hanging out in a room with newborns on the weekend my child was due would not have been wise. While my situation was not anyone else's fault, I did not need to put myself in a situation where the pain was too much or the temptation to be ugly might be greater than I could realistically control at the time.

There will always be a segment of the population that simply doesn't understand what the mother who has lost is experiencing and that is okay. There is no need to try to force them to understand or to take out our pain on them. It's okay to not be okay when triggered, but it's not okay to stay not okay forever. Good friends can be a tremendous source of support, and there may be seasons to get assistance from professional counselors to work through the grieving and healing process.

I remember having a friend who had struggled for many years to conceive and was so excited when it was confirmed that she was finally pregnant. Sadly, she lost the baby very soon after that. She was devastated. Most people couldn't understand why she was reacting as she was given it was such a short pregnancy. Because of my background, I could empathize and understood that as soon as she had learned she was pregnant she had emotionally attached, probably had name options chosen, had imagined the baby's room fully decorated, envisioned the first day of kindergarten and perhaps dreamed of graduation. Her grief was much greater than even what I experienced with the loss of my first or second.

The depth of her grief was directly correlated to the depth of her bond, and she had bonded very deeply very quickly with this child. All of those dreams she had for the child were now gone and she had to process the grief of losing those dreams. She eventually did go on to successfully carry natural children and it is women like her who, when they successfully deliver children, royally mess up my mascara. The happy tears simply overflow.

THE DEPTH OF HER GRIEF WAS DIRECTLY CORRELATED TO THE DEPTH OF HER BOND, AND SHE HAD BONDED VERY DEEPLY VERY QUICKLY WITH THIS CHILD

It was not long before I conceived for the third time. While I had been in Taiwan, it seemed like every typical food they gave me was somehow considered to be good for fertility. I'm not sure I see the connection between fertility and small fish with their heads still on, pig ears, quail eggs, chicken feet, squid pizza, or any of the other unique "delicacies" I "enjoyed." Had the infamous black chicken actually done the trick? I'm not one to put much stock in those random superstitions but I could joke that perhaps

God used all of that food I had never had before—and some of which I hope to never have again—to shock my system enough to make something work.

I FELT MORE COMFORTABLE IN THE LAND OF DISAPPOINTMENT BECAUSE I KNEW WHAT THAT FELT LIKE

Would this baby actually make it to my arms? As messed up as it sounds, I felt more comfortable in the land of disappointment because I knew what that felt like. It was very hard to be excited and allow myself to get my hopes up because "what if." It would be new and unfamiliar territory to carry a pregnancy successfully.

I was now getting into still higher risk categories. I was over 30 and had a history of miscarriages. When the doctor couldn't pick up the heartbeat in the office one day, she was wise to order an immediate ultrasound. Even if the baby was fine, having mom wait for any duration of time could easily put mom in an emotional tailspin. Yes, 2 Corinthians 10:5 says that we are to "take every thought captive to the obedience of Christ," but sometimes that's easier said than done. Sometimes part of taking thoughts captive is allowing God's truth to come through the God-given talents of medical professionals and technology.

With my strong pro-life background, I had seen many ultrasounds and without the technician saying anything I would likely be able to see, at least at a basic or obvious level, if things were good. At this particular appointment I could not see the screen, so I was dependent on my husband and the ultrasound technician for feedback. As my husband stood there looking at the screen, his countenance communicated that this would be my third strikeout. The technician had read the chart, knew my history, and knew why I was there. I forgive him for breaking the rules as he turned to my husband and said, "I'm not supposed to say anything, but there are the arms; there are the legs; and there is the heartbeat." My husband looked at him in disbelief. The last time he had barely seen more than a little flashing light. The technician's response was priceless. "They only have nine months to get this done so they have to move quickly."

Things progressed just fine for the baby but there were times when mom wasn't fine. My mental and emotional map was more conditioned to handling loss than success and there were plenty of times I would have myself in ridiculous tailspins of worry. If there is one thing I finally did learn, it was that having the nurses' desk at the doctors' office on speed dial was the best remedy. They were the trained professional voices of reason who could talk me off the ledge of worry.

I remember giving counsel to a pregnant woman who had walked a similar path and was in tears fearing she was going to lose yet another baby. She was convinced she was crazy for being like this all the time. I had to be honest with her. She was completely normal given her background. Hormones can mess with us during pregnancy but even more than that our history can mess with us. Bringing the nurse's clarity of truth could fix her mental state in an instant. Her baby was just fine and eventually arrived happy and healthy.

As mid-November 2005 rolled around, I was a mess. I had a D&E for my first baby on my step daughter's birthday and a D&E

scheduled but then done the day before Navo's birthday. The only child's birthday left was Mila's. I wouldn't be able to handle it if I lost this baby too and it fell on her birthday. Fortunately, her birthday came and went without incident.

The baby was due in late May but around 4:00 in the morning on May 10, my water broke. After sending Mila and Navo off to school, we headed to the hospital. I wasn't sensing any real urgency because as of yet this was nothing like the movies. If I was having contractions they weren't bothering me. It wasn't long after we arrived at the hospital that I looked at the nurses and said the race is on. I knew a woman in Wisconsin who was expecting a baby girl and she had told me that she was going to be induced on May 10. "Wouldn't that be funny," I thought, "if we both had our babies the same day?"

My water may have broken but it really didn't seem like my body wanted to let this baby come out, so they started the medications to speed up contractions. The nurse would ask me from time to time if I wanted the epidural and I assured her I was fine. I wasn't necessarily comfortable but it is childbirth and I didn't really expect it to be without some level of discomfort.

I had thought it was funny when they asked me to put together a childbirth plan several weeks ahead of time. I didn't know what to expect since it was my first time, and I sure wasn't naïve enough to think the baby would completely cooperate with whatever my plan might be. Somehow I don't think my paternal grandmother ever wrote out a childbirth plan after attending a multi-week class, although perhaps she was schooled in real life by helping friends or relatives deliver. She successfully delivered nine children at home of whom seven made it to adulthood. If she got through it at home, I felt pretty confident that the doctor and team of nurses could get me through this just fine. As for my plan with the epidural, I told the doctor, "I'd like to go natural but there may come a point in time when either I decide, or you decide, that the right thing for me will be the drugs." By late afternoon, I decided the right thing for me was the drugs. One minute was "this isn't the most enjoyable experience, but I'm okay" and the next was "Oh my God, this is like the movies. I think I'm going to die. Eve, I'm really mad at you right now!" Genesis 3:26 was definitely accurate, "I will make your pains in childbearing very severe; with painful labor you will give birth to children." I am exceedingly thankful for the grace of modern medicine and the anesthesiologist became my instant best friend.

Apparently, my mother was six hours start to finish with me, and the doctor played catch with my brother. The doctor told my dad he would likely have to deliver the third himself, and thus, there was no third. I was definitely not following her pattern, and my father asked my mother in jest if she had forgotten to teach me how this was done. I was taking entirely too long. It was almost twenty hours start to finish and just before midnight, a little healthy baby girl came into my life (and yes, my friend in Wisconsin delivered the same day.)

Everyone had been convinced I was having a boy. I had a dream a few weeks earlier and woke up thinking, "What if it's a girl?" We can't name her Caleb. It was a bit of a toss-up between Leah and Lydia, but ultimately, I was particularly drawn to the name Lydia because of the woman in the book of Acts—a businesswoman who was hospitable to missionaries. Lydia Faith had arrived.

Chapter 11
Joy Comes in the Morning

I wish I could say that with Lydia's arrival there was much rejoicing all around, but that would not be the case. Though most of the family members in the hospital were very happy, one was not, and it was very apparent. I was probably the only one in the room who could have foreseen Mila's reaction. She wanted this to be a baby boy. A baby sister was going to be a trigger for her. Would I keep this new little sister and get rid of her? While she was legally adopted that didn't make her feel any more secure. Her biological mother had abandoned her after the arrival of her half-sister. Maybe I would abandon her also. In her heart there was still a fear of rejection, and the fact that this was a little girl made the flashback to her younger half-sister that much more difficult. I wanted to be excited for my new baby but wanted to be sensitive to her also. I felt caught in the middle.

To put it mildly, Mila was not being very nice. She was verbally lashing out. I didn't like it, but there wasn't much I could do. It didn't matter what words I would say. She would have to see in action that I would not reject her. The issue was in her heart and would take time to work through. I had the closest bond with her and could handle her outbursts better than everyone else. She was pushing all of my mother's buttons and now my mother was really mad. I'm sure the nurses were wondering what that loud unpleasant family drama was down the hall.

We were now well into the wee hours of the morning when everyone left. I had to stay in the hospital and couldn't go home and be the calming voice for Mila. I needed to do something and chose to call on my backup team. It was in the early hours of the morning that I left a message on the voicemail of the guidance counselor at school. One of the true advantages of having my children in a small Christian school was that they knew our family well and knew the children well. The teachers and staff could be stand-ins for me when needed, and at this point, I needed them to keep a watchful eye on Mila. I needed them to speak love and acceptance into her heart. She had arrived in the family before this child. I had legally adopted her. I was not going to reject her.

By her next visit to the hospital, Mila had calmed down considerably. While she still wasn't particularly happy about the situation, she was choosing to accept it. She eventually grew to absolutely adore Lydia. Lydia was like her little human doll. I think it's fair to say that Mila can be held responsible for the fact that Lydia learned to walk by nine months. Big sister was always holding her up on her feet and trying to walk her around. Her little legs grew strong and seemed to know exactly what to do. Lydia became the adorable micro toddler running around in the church lobby on Sunday mornings.

Chapter 12
He is the Great Redeemer

───────────────────

"Forget the former things; do not dwell on the past. See, I am doing a new thing! Now it springs up; do you not perceive it? I am making a way in the wilderness and streams in the wasteland."

ISAIAH 43:18- 19

God is a Great Redeemer and He can redeem anything.

Lydia was in the car seat on my lap as the kind senior citizen volunteer pushed me in the wheelchair to the front door of the hospital. I was suddenly completely overcome with emotion and tears were running down my face. The volunteer asked if I was okay, and I explained how twice before I had been pushed to those very same doors with empty arms. On this beautiful spring day, I now had a precious newborn baby girl with me. God was allowing those difficult memories to come to the surface and be replaced. I would no longer have to associate those doors with loss. He was allowing a deep wound to reopen so He could show His incredible redemptive love and heal the wound from the inside out. He had taken me to a very specific physical place to create a good memory that replaced the old painful memories.

This was not the first time God had redeemed my memories associated with a place. I remember as a single person going to the beach with a group of friends. The particular beach they had chosen was one that was not filled with happy memories for me. The group consensus was to eat at a particular restaurant which also stirred up unpleasant memories. In the way that only God can do He reached deep into my heart and healed childhood wounds using a gang of friends, a silly game of co-ed football on a cold empty beach, and a pizza with sweet peppers of all things. I've read countless other stories of God redeeming places and memories in ways that simply defy human explanation. He is infinitely creative and nothing is beyond Him.

God can also redeem dates on a calendar and there is a redemption story in God's choice of the day for Lydia's birth. She was not due until late May and Mother's Day that year fell on May 14. Mother's Day was always hard on many levels. Mila and Navo were torn. While I was "mom," their biological mom was out there somewhere. It was a day of mixed emotions for them. I tried to be sensitive to them and didn't get upset if the day came and went without much fanfare. Mother's Day church services only added to the difficulty. It was the day they chose to do baby dedications and it was hard to watch all of those families up front with their adorable babies remembering the two I lost and not knowing if I would ever have one of my own. Even though I had my adopted children there was a part of me that also wanted a natural child. God saw to it that Lydia would arrive in time for her first church service to be on Mother's Day. God was clearly showing me that not only is He a redeemer of lives and places I could add redeemer of dates on the calendar.

I was content with this one baby unless God wanted to give me more. Not long after Lydia turned one, something didn't seem right and I realized, as I was having a very early miscarriage, that I had conceived again. I did not have a chance to emotionally bond with this baby, so this was by far the easiest miscarriage to navigate. It did make me wonder if perhaps I could have another child.

> I WAS CONTENT WITH THIS ONE BABY UNLESS GOD WANTED TO GIVE ME MORE

God wasn't done adding children to my world and I conceived yet again. I was considered high risk but things moved along just fine with this baby. I was working a distance from our house and there were many jokes about who was going to drive me to the hospital if I went into labor at the office. This child already had quite a following from the performance in the conference room one day. I was sitting still but the baby was anything but still. There was a massive stretch with feet braced on my ribs which definitely caught my attention as nerves were pinched between a foot and my bones. There was then a sweeping roll from one side to the other which was noticed by a woman sitting across from me. She let out an audible "Oh my goodness!" which made everyone turn. As if on cue, there was an encore rollback. Everyone sat there stunned at the visible display of life growing inside me. Little feet, knees, elbows, fists or whatever were stretching, moving and appeared as very obvious protruding bumps that went from one side to the other. I wasn't just carrying a neat little ball on the front. I was carrying a wiggly little person who appeared ready to pop right out and say hello. Lydia had been known to knock a hacky sack off my stomach to the delight of two Japanese exchange students, but this baby was outdoing her shows.

The baby was due to arrive in late February, but by the grace of God he came early. On Friday morning, February 6, I went to a doctor's appointment and it was apparent that delivery would likely be sooner rather than later. I decided I would continue on to the office that afternoon, but also let everyone know I could be having the baby over the weekend. Monday morning I was still pregnant and wisely opted to work from home. I was emailing back and forth with one of the guys at the office on some budget issues and shortly before 5:00 felt an incredible pain. I emailed in that if that was a contraction there would likely be a baby tonight. Almost a moment later there was another shooting pain and I decided it was worth going to the hospital. Of course when I arrived the pains stopped. Given I was reasonably dilated they opted to let me stay. I wasn't due for another two weeks but I had been early with the first so likely all would be fine with this one.

This time the doctor advised me to get the drugs even though I felt I was doing okay. She was concerned that we might wait too long and I wouldn't be able to get them. Hindsight after delivering a very large baby would prove she made the right decision.

As we were getting later into the evening I looked at the clock and realized it was very likely this baby would go past midnight and be born on February 10, exactly four years to the day after my second D&E. The very doctor who had told me it was unlikely I would have natural children without intervention was about to deliver my second natural child. In God's sovereignty, Caleb was born on the morning of February 10, 2009.

Interestingly, that date would come back again later in a bittersweet way. On February 10, 2015, we celebrated Caleb's sixth birthday. My mother was living with us and participated in the festivities. After the children went to bed she mentioned that she wasn't feeling that well. She said something about the light seeming different in the room and made a comment wondering if this is what her mother felt like before she died. At the time, I thought she was being a little dramatic. She spoke on the phone to the nurse practitioner on call and a little while later asked me to call an ambulance. The first team arrived and a second was called to assist. She was talking to them but then started losing consciousness. Every light was on in the house and there was lots of commotion. Amazingly the children never heard anything. As the first ambulance left, the driver of the second said very plainly, "We almost lost her in your foyer, and we may still lose her tonight."

I called my brother and we both headed to the hospital. When we arrived they sent a chaplain out to get us. Obviously, that didn't seem like it was going to be good news. One of the doctors came in and explained that she arrived at the hospital and at 11:30 went into full cardiac arrest. They had tried to bring her back for 45 minutes with no success and declared her dead at 12:15. I was in shock but also very much at peace. She had been having some health issues but nothing that I thought was pointing to this. I had been concerned about the inability of some leg wounds to heal and that perhaps at some point they might say diabetes. What if they had to amputate her feet? She was significantly overweight and there was no way I would be able to care for her in our home. She would not handle moving into any type of institutional care well. I surely didn't want anything horrible to happen and for my young children to be the ones to find her.

God had just taken her in the most merciful way possible for all of us. As my brother and I sat there with the chaplain in those wee hours of the morning, it occurred to me that really her heart stopped on February 10. I reframed the events in my mind and decided that she wasn't done partying for the day. She had been there for Caleb's party and wanted to make it in time to participate in the "heavenly" birthday party with my daughter. She was a bit of a stubborn woman, so in my mind it didn't matter how good that emergency room team was, she was going to heaven that night to be part of her granddaughter's party!

Chapter 13
Blessed to be a Blessing

❦────────────────────❧

"Give and it will be given to you. A good measure,
pressed down, shaken together, and running over..."

LUKE 6:38A

When Lydia was born, I was determined to follow the guidance of the American Academy of Pediatrics and breastfeed as long as possible. She would not latch well and when she was three days old, we realized after I bought a breast pump that she was simply not getting enough milk. All of her fussiness was because of hunger. The breast pump traveled with me everywhere so I could make sure to give her the very best nourishment I possibly could. By the time she was six months old, my body was barely producing anything. The doctor kept assuring me she would be fine and that I had gone above and beyond the call of duty in trying as hard as I had. Most women would pump only when they weren't around their baby, otherwise they were direct nursing. Not many women would put themselves through the hassle of exclusively pumping only to have to bottle feed their child. None of her words of encouragement helped. I felt like a failure as a mother. I had gone through so much to finally have Lydia and wanted to do my absolute best, but my best wasn't good enough.

Caleb began the journey that would redeem that memory. When Caleb arrived, he too would not latch well, so I immediately started pumping in the hospital. I was not going to wait three days to discover he was hungry. Even at two weeks early he was a full two pounds larger than Lydia had been at birth. He was a very large baby, and it had been a tough delivery. I was exhausted and had a lot of physical healing to do. I knew I would be going home to two teenagers and a toddler. Unfortunately, I was not going to have a standard maternity leave from work and would need to have the energy to work from home. I needed rest and tried to lean on the nurses as much as possible for those few days in the hospital. I pumped for him and took the bottle down to the nursery area. The nurse took it and had a sort of puzzled look on her face as she asked if I had just pumped that whole bottle. I assured her I had and that was the end of that. What I didn't realize was that was the foreshadowing of what was to come.

The day I was discharged we had to swing by the back surgeon's office. My husband was going to have outpatient surgery the following week. The nurses noticed I still had my hospital bracelet on and yes, I confirmed that the baby in the car seat was just days old. Caleb was just a week old when we were taking daddy in for his surgery. The doctor looked at me at one point and asked if I was okay. I thought I was fine other than being obviously tired with a newborn. I headed over to my mother's house because she was going to watch Caleb while I went to a quick church board meeting. I returned to my mom's house to wait there until it was time to pick up my husband at the hospital. It would be a lot easier to pump and feed Caleb there than hunting for a place in the hospital. Eventually, they called and said they had decided to keep my husband overnight. They wanted to get his pain meds regulated and felt I had more than enough to handle with a newborn. The surgeon didn't feel comfortable sending him home for me to handle on my own, and I think he probably saw something developing in me but didn't push it after I said I was fine.

That night, I started running a fever and could barely take care of me, let alone a newborn. I went into a period of every other day spiking fevers. My doctor felt pretty sure I was having engorgement issues. I just needed to pump more often.

When I brought Caleb home, I would pump and bottle feed him. Sometimes he wasn't hungry but I felt I needed to pump. That was okay. I could freeze the milk for when I didn't have enough. Sometimes I would pump and there would be more than he could drink. Again, I could freeze the excess.

I also seemed to have an issue with the pump that I had not had when I was pumping for Lydia. There were times that the bottles that came standard with the pump would get very full. If I wasn't paying attention they would overflow, which was really quite annoying. Fortunately, I was able to find some larger bottles from another manufacturer with screw threads that were just close enough to the same size as those on the stock standard bottles and helped solve the overflow inconveniences. On some occasions, even those larger bottles could overflow.

I kept wondering when I would not have enough milk for Caleb and would have to start dipping into the stash in the freezer. A time of lack in supply never seemed to come. The kitchen freezer was filling up, so I moved some to the small drop-in freezer. The drop-in freezer was rapidly filling up. There were more people than just Caleb in the house, and we needed space in the freezer for more than just breastmilk. I was becoming desperate and started searching everywhere for someone who could use the extra milk. I remembered the feelings of failure I felt when I couldn't provide for Lydia and there had to be someone out there who would need or want the milk.

I eventually ended up calling a milk bank in North Carolina, who for the practical reason of shipping costs, directed me to Ohio. I went through the lifestyle screening and blood testing process to become approved and began shipping box after box of milk to the Mother's Milk Bank of Ohio in Columbus. It took a little while until they caught on to my level of overproduction. At one hundred ounces a day, I was not common but not unheard of. The milk bank became a blessing for me in that I didn't have to try to moderate the supply and risk drying up and not providing for Caleb. I was a blessing to them because I had a routine supply for them to distribute to the various NICUs and other families who needed the milk.

At that time, the milk bank only accepted donors for a year because the mother's milk changes as her baby grows and their primary recipients were the smallest NICU babies who needed the higher fat content milk. As I finished out the year, I started looking for another outlet for the extra milk. I found a very health-conscious mom whose adopted child had been born to a drug-using mother. Not only were she and her husband vegan, I was pretty sure if they didn't grow it on their own property they were not going to eat it. When the doctor told her to give the baby over the counter formula you can likely guess how well that advice was received. She cut a deal with the doctor to give her thirty days of trying things her way and if the baby was not in better shape after the thirty days she would do it his way. Several donor moms stepped up to support her, and thirty days later the doctor looked at her baby and asked where she was getting that stuff because he had several other patients who needed it. Obviously, her son was thriving on the donor milk. As we were closing in on her son's first birthday, I had to stop pumping because God was sending another baby my way. Pumping could confuse my body about where the baby was and could initiate a miscarriage.

It was another rather uneventful pregnancy, although I did start off with lots of trips to the specialists because of my "advanced maternal age." One morning as I was approaching my due date, I woke up in unbelievable pain that wouldn't stop. I got a shower and had hoped to get all of the children off to school before heading to the hospital. At this point, Mila was off in the Marines so I just had Navo, Lydia and Caleb at home. Within a little while, the pain was getting the best of me and thus, everything became about me. I called Navo's school and told them he might be late because he had to take his young siblings to daycare. I was headed to the hospital to have a baby. I called the doctor's office and they said they would page the doctor on call. When she called me back I was polite but said I didn't care when I saw her. I wanted the anesthesiologist to meet me at the front door. She called ahead to the hospital and told them to not even triage me but send me directly to labor and delivery. I was the rational woman who took hours before wanting the drugs with the first one, let her recommend them the second time, and now was begging for them and hadn't yet arrived at the hospital. She was pretty sure I was having a baby that day.

Once at the hospital, the nurse put the monitor on and could see why I was so animated. I was having very strong contractions with no break in between. I was dehydrated and they would have to fix that before I could get the epidural. I had a solution for them. Put the IV in and forget the dripping nonsense, switch it to firehose. Give me a 32-ounce bottle of water. I'll chug it. Just get me that epidural! Finally, the nurse called for the anesthesiologist. I was keenly aware of everything going on and was wondering where he was. They eventually had to "fess up." He got called away for an emergency cesarean. I was okay with the mother getting my drugs, but that baby was in trouble with me. After what seemed like an eternity, the friendly anesthesiologist came in and overrode those rebellious nerves that kept screaming pain. While I was now a calm patient, they were becoming concerned for the baby. The massive contractions were putting a great deal of pressure on the baby and the baby's heart rate was extremely high. They debated about doing an emergency cesarean, but opted to let me continue. When it was finally time to push, he was ready. In less than fifteen minutes, Joshua was out. He gets to hold the record for my fastest delivery, and as with the others, I started pumping for him while in the hospital.

Shortly before Joshua arrived, I had reached out to the milk bank as a heads up in case it would be another overproducing adventure. Sure enough, I was back to the regular trips to the FedEx office with boxes of frozen milk. With Joshua, I was able to donate a little bit longer because they had determined that since they now had the technology to test the fat content of the milk, they knew exactly what the NICU babies were receiving and could use the fortifiers if needed. At the end of August 2012, I again retired the breast pump. Joshua was almost eighteen months old and Mila had just delivered her son, my new grandchild. It seemed like it was time for me to be finished.

On September 6, 2012, I received an email from the Mother's Milk Bank of Ohio. In the email the director wrote, "The last milk you sent was sent to Children's Hospital of Philadelphia." Those words seemed to jump off the screen and overwhelmed me with emotion.

Approximately seventeen years earlier, I was fresh out of college and working for a large accounting firm in Philadelphia. I was assigned to the audit for the Children's Hospital of Philadelphia (CHOP). CHOP had put in a new NICU unit and we needed to audit all of the expenditures related to that addition. It was a very impressive state-of-the-art facility, and they wanted to show it off. We were taken on a tour to see the new facilities.

All of the high tech equipment was hidden behind panels on the wall. At the push of a button, they could bring out the life-saving equipment. With it tucked behind the walls, the room didn't seem intimidating. There were rocking chairs and other amenities that made you forget this room would be home to the most fragile infants fighting for their lives.

I was okay with seeing the new NICU because there weren't any babies in the room. I was simply looking at equipment, and there is nothing emotional in that. Our tour guide then suggested taking us to see the older facility. If the babies weren't here in the new area that meant they were there in the old area. I really didn't want to go. Reality and emotion would be staring me in the face down there.

It was very difficult for me to see the babies in the NICU. I am naturally wired to want to help or fix. As I stood there looking at the babies and the parents, I couldn't help or fix anything. I could see the anguish in the faces of the parents who were hoping and praying that somehow through time and the team of medical professionals, God would deliver a miracle to their child. On some very limited level, God was allowing me to feel what those parents were feeling. That experience significantly impacted me. My heart wanted an answer. "Why, God, would you allow me to see that when there's nothing I can do?" It was a highly emotional question that would have no answer for many years.

IT WAS VERY DIFFICULT FOR ME TO SEE THE BABIES IN THE NICU

As I read that email from the milk bank and saw the "Children's Hospital of Philadelphia," I was completely overwhelmed with emotion and tears began flowing. I had been giving all of that milk to the milk bank for the NICU babes without ever consciously associating it with that experience in my early twenties. It wasn't until I read that email that it all came flooding back and I had the realization that God had never forgotten my heart's desire to do something for those babies and their parents. He had chosen to fulfill my heart's desire and answer that prayer in His own timing and in a way that I could never have imagined or planned.

I had retired the breast pump the weekend Mila gave birth to her son. I would be coming up on 40 and it was probably time for me to be done with babies … only I wasn't. I soon learned there was another little one on the way.

With Nathaniel, I once again was momma cow—a term that was a running joke in our family and never had any negative connotations. In fact, I once joked with the associate pastor of the church I had attended for so many years because as a young child I had spent a summer on his dairy farm and perhaps something had rubbed off on me. Once again, I would be supporting NICU babies and the Mother's Milk Bank of Ohio. Once again, I made weekly trips to the FedEx office late in the evening so the milk would arrive still frozen the next morning.

One day, I received a text message that was prefaced with "I feel really awkward asking this …" The older sister of one of Mila's high school friends had received a call from her close friend who had just had a baby. The baby was in for a routine visit and was being flagged for failure to thrive. The doctor was very concerned. The baby was losing weight and it seemed her mom could not produce enough milk for her. Mila's friend's sister went to her mother asking if she would please contact me to see if there was any chance I had any milk I could give to this baby. It would be an awkward request, but after thinking about it for a little while, she felt that God wanted her to at least pass the request along. I remember what it was like to feel like a failure as a mother when I couldn't provide breastmilk for my child and there was no question that I would help this mother. I could have milk to her the next morning.

Some babies won't take another mother's milk but this little one did. This little girl started gaining weight and the doctor was pleased. We began a long relationship of milk runs that carried her well past her first birthday.

I don't know why I struggled with milk for Lydia but was overly blessed with the boys. I can say only this: God knew that the season of lack would build a heart that could steward the excess and do whatever it took to get milk to children in need when it was needed.

God always orchestrated the relationships for donor milk in convenient locations. The two long-term relationships ended up being with mothers who lived between my house and my office, even though I had different employers with each of them. I could make daily morning or evening runs, and it wasn't out of my way to do so. I was even blessed to find moms in other states when business travel took me to places that involved airline flights. It was convenient to be able to meet up in a Starbucks parking lot before heading to an airport. I could bless a mom and avoid challenges with the Transportation Security Administration. Because I had been screened pretty heavily by the milk bank, I was a lower risk donor than just some other random stranger.

To some people, the whole idea of being a milk donor or sharing milk may seem really strange, but it's really just a modern-day version of the wet nurse of Bible times. Before formula, the options for a mother who was unable to nurse on her own would have been very limited and finding a wet nurse would have been critical. If a mother died in childbirth, a family would have needed to reach out to a relative with a young child or look for another unrelated woman to nurse the baby.

In Exodus 2, Moses' mother was paid to nurse her own son on behalf of Pharaoh's daughter. Isn't that just like God to take care of the mother who was forced to give up her child to save him?

> *Now a man of the tribe of Levi married a Levite woman, and she became pregnant and gave birth to a son. When she saw that he was a fine child, she hid him for three months. But when she could hide him no longer, she got a papyrus basket for him and coated it with tar and pitch. Then she placed the child in it and put it among the reeds along the bank of the Nile. His sister stood at a distance to see what would happen to him. Then Pharaoh's daughter went down to the Nile to bathe, and her attendants were walking along the*

riverbank. She saw the basket among the reeds and sent her female slave to get it. She opened it and saw the baby. He was crying, and she felt sorry for him. "This is one of the Hebrew babies," she said. Then his sister asked Pharaoh's daughter, "Shall I go and get one of the Hebrew women to nurse the baby for you?" "Yes, go," she answered. So the girl went and got the baby's mother. Pharaoh's daughter said to her, "Take this baby and nurse him for me, and I will pay you." So the woman took the baby and nursed him. When the child grew older, she took him to Pharaoh's daughter and he became her son. She named him Moses, saying, "I drew him out of the water."

(EXODUS 2:1-10, NIV)

Being an overproducer had its benefits. I was able to get back into my regular clothes very soon after the birth of my children, and I was able to eat as much as I wanted without gaining weight because my metabolism was so incredibly high. There were some drawbacks. At peak production, I would have to pump every two to three hours around the clock. Constantly disrupted sleep does take a toll on your body. It also meant I had to take the pump with me everywhere I went and sometimes had to pump in inconvenient places. There was an element of sacrifice on my part to do what was required to support the production that I was simply donating to the milk banks and various other moms, but it is a sacrifice that I would gladly make all over again.

I look at being a milk donor as a unique take on this scripture: "Then the righteous will answer him, 'Lord, when did we see you hungry and feed you, or thirsty and give you something to drink?' ... The King will reply, 'Truly I tell you, whatever you did for one of the least of these brothers and sisters of mine, you did for me.'" Matthew 25:37, 40

In working with the milk banks, I learned a great deal about the benefits of breastmilk for premature babies. "Evidence demonstrates that formula-fed infants are at a heightened risk of developing NEC [necrotizing enterocolitis], while an exclusive human milk diet offers these infants the most protection. When mother's own milk is unavailable for premature infants, pasteurized donor breast milk is the next best option."[1]

Of course, it's easy to read about the benefits of breastmilk for premature babies and have a head knowledge of it, but it becomes real when it hits your heart. I was blessed to meet the adopted daughter of a family friend. When I heard her story it gave me the concrete realization that being a donor mom was worth way more than the minor inconveniences I was experiencing. This little girl was born prematurely, and unfortunately, developed necrotizing enterocolitis which destroyed her small intestines. Her biological mother abandoned her at the hospital, and this family friend with specialized nursing skills adopted her. This young lady faces life long challenges because of her rough start. There are several emergency room trips each year and rounds with feeding tubes and specialized diets because she can't absorb nutrients like the rest of us. Her adoptive mom and dad are amazing for pushing through the challenges with her. It is not an easy road.

If my sleepless nights and other "inconveniences" over the course of a few years prevented even one baby from developing NEC then they were all worth it. There is nothing that I went through as an "inconvenience" that comes close to what the NICU babies and their families go through. I would gladly do it all again.

> *Remember this: Whoever sows sparingly will also reap sparingly, and whoever sows generously will also reap generously. Each of you should give what you have decided in your heart to give, not reluctantly or under compulsion, for God loves a cheerful giver. And God is able to bless you abundantly, so that in all things at all times, having all that you need, you will abound in every good work.*

> 2 CORINTHIANS 9-6-8

ENDNOTE

1. https://necsociety.org/2014/04/12/the-best-childrens-hospitals-use-donor-milk/.

Chapter 14
To Announce or Not to Announce

When Mila gave birth to her son, I was pretty sure I was done having babies. Weeks later I learned that I was expecting Nathaniel. I was now going to be having a child past the age of 40. I had been considered high risk with my earlier pregnancies because of the patterns of loss and my ever-increasing age. Now it was definitely not a question. I was in the high-risk category.

I was assigned a perinatologist who specializes in maternal-fetal medicine. At the first ultrasound, the doctor expressed some concern because the baby showed some of the markers that suggest Down Syndrome. I was given some options for additional testing. All of my pro-life knowledge gained from listening to Dr. Willkie during my teen years helped me understand what was involved in some of the testing options and whether there would be risks to the baby. Some of the tests did have risks, and I would not risk the baby's life for those tests. There were other newer tests that would not risk the health of the baby, but they would not necessarily be conclusive and could bring back incorrect results. I ultimately chose to wait to see what future ultrasounds would show. Those would be agonizing weeks waiting and wondering.

HEARING THAT MY BABY MAY HAVE DOWN SYNDROME WAS NOT THE NEWS I WANTED TO HEAR

Hearing that my baby may have Down Syndrome was not the news I wanted to hear, but I was willing to accept it. God would not give me a child whom He also would not give me the ability to parent. He had given me a challenging one in Mila, and He brought me through. He could bring me through again if needed.

I knew I would not terminate the pregnancy, but I was hesitant to say anything to anyone about being pregnant. With questions about the condition of the baby yet unanswered, I wasn't ready to be excited. If I began saying anything, others would likely pick up on my own reservations, and I didn't want to have to answer questions I wasn't ready to answer. I knew I would love the baby, but would I struggle with being excited for his or her birth. How would I handle the reactions of my family and friends if I announced I was pregnant with a baby who had Down Syndrome? I needed to resolve these issues in my own heart before I was willing to deal with anyone else's. I would not want my convictions to be swayed by anyone else. In the case of Mila, I felt God gave me a very clear mandate to be her mother, and I had a heart-level conviction that could not be shaken. I would need to have a similar heart-level conviction for carrying and parenting this child. I needed to process the preliminary diagnosis in front of me, come to terms with it, and develop my convictions.

I know families with special needs children and their children are a blessing. If this child was born with special needs, I was confident he or she would be a blessing to us. God doesn't make mistakes and thus, nothing about this child would be a mistake. He or she was being made in the image of God within my womb. God still had a plan and purpose for him or her.

I came to the realization that if in fact this baby had Down Syndrome, the first significant change would be in how I prepared for his or her arrival. I made the mental list of who I was going to call for advice on preparing for a special child. I knew the local organizations I was going to reach out to for advice and guidance. I was aware of organizations in my area which address needs of special children and others which support families in their unique challenges of parenting their special children. I was personally acquainted with an organization that assists challenged adults and could help me with long term planning and realistic expectations for natural potential, keeping in mind that I still believe in miracles. I know parents of special children whom I greatly respect for how they have worked with their children to bring out the very best in them. Their children are performing at levels beyond natural expectations, and I believe it is directly a result of their efforts to remove barriers for their children and get them the assistance and resources that could help them progress as far as possible. These would be the people I would trust for good counsel and the wisdom gained through personal experience. There was one thing I knew for sure—this child would come into the world to a mom who had done everything she possibly could to prepare for him or her.

There were numerous ultrasounds before the doctor felt pretty confident that the baby did not have Down Syndrome. In the meantime, I had stalled as long as I possibly could to tell people I was expecting. Perhaps to be more accurate, I should say I stalled well beyond things becoming very obvious to finally be verbally honest and admit I was pregnant. Baggy sweatshirts and fleeces can only hide so much for so long. My body had been stretched three times before, and I always carried the "basketball" on the front, so thinking I could hide this was really quite delusional. When asked why I had tried to hide being pregnant for so long at times, I had to explain the reasons above.

Because of my "advanced" age, the doctor did not want me going too long. So, if the baby didn't arrive before a certain point, they would induce me. I had scheduled the induction around the rest of my calendar, and it was finally time. Apparently, several other babies decided it was their time to come also, and the hospital got three of us at once. I was more than happy to let the other moms jump ahead of me for assistance. They were obviously in much more discomfort, and I remember what it was like with Joshua when I wanted everything to be about helping me. I would gladly wait my turn and let the nurses tend to those moms before starting my induction.

NO TWO DELIVERIES WERE THE SAME, BUT GIVEN THIS WOULD BE MY FOURTH, I FULLY EXPECTED THIS TO BE MY FASTEST

No two deliveries were the same, but given this would be my fourth, I fully expected this to be my fastest. I like to say that Nathaniel decided he was so excited to see me that he wanted to be able to look at my face as soon as he came out. Coming out face up, unfortunately, just slowed down the process. Oh well, he was here and healthy.

As with all of my pregnancies, we had opted for the gender reveal to occur in the delivery room. When Lydia was finally allowed to come into the hospital room to meet her newest sibling she was upset. She didn't want Nathaniel. She wanted Victoria. It was a flashback to when she was born and Mila wanted Caleb, not Lydia. I had to tell Lydia that her big sister had a very similar reaction when she was born and reminded her how much big sister grew to love her. I was sure she would grow to love Nathaniel. By her next visit, she had warmed up to the idea of another little brother and was happy to hold him.

GOD DOESN'T
MAKE MISTAKES
AND THUS,
NOTHING ABOUT
THIS CHILD
WOULD BE A
MISTAKE

Chapter 15
What's in a Name

⌁───────────────────⌁

While doing some work in the Chicago area, I had the opportunity to briefly meet a lovely family. They have several children, and one has obvious medical challenges. When I heard their story, all I could think of was, "Death and life are in the power of the tongue: and they that love it shall eat the fruit thereof" (Proverbs 18:21). This family had named their challenged daughter Liv, not short for Olivia as I initially thought, just Liv. I didn't even have to ask the next obvious question because they were ready to share the reason why. They named her Liv because they wanted every person who came in contact with their daughter to proclaim life over her. It really would sound wrong to make the statement, "Liv is going to die." I absolutely love the wisdom they used in choosing her name. They, and everyone who comes in contact with Liv, are using the power of their tongue to bless her with life.

Obviously, when a child is born the parents get to select a name just as Liv's family had done with her. When a child comes to a family through adoption, they likely arrive with a name. An adopting family has the opportunity to change all or part of their name. Our children were ages eight and nine when they came to live with us. By the time of their actual adoption, they were eleven and twelve, so they were already well established with their names. Because Mila was twelve, she was required by Pennsylvania law to consent to the adoption. She was also pretty vocal that she didn't want her name changed. Eventually, she did accept what we chose to do. Neither Mila nor Navo were given middle names at birth, so we simply shifted their original last name to a middle name and tacked on a new last name. They did not need to give up any of their original name.

We don't really know anything about the origin of Navo's name. In some respects, it may have been almost prophetic in that he joined the Navy. I also like to think his name could be treated more as the acronym for Noble Artistic Victorious Overcomer. Mila's biological mother wanted to name her Milagro which in Spanish means "miracle," but may have been unsure how to spell it, so shortened it to Mila. When I think back to the Mila that came to live with us and the Mila many years later—she is a walking miracle.

In those early days, one of our neighbors was a police officer. He had definitely seen his share of disastrous lives throughout his career. He knew the path that Mila was on during her troublesome start with us would not lead to a good place. By the time we moved away, he had seen a remarkable transformation. Much like "Liv," on some small level, every time we spoke Mila's name we were declaring a miracle for her.

When choosing the names for our natural children we would be intentional and the significance would center on the character traits of several Biblical heroes. With each child's birth, there had to be two names ready because the gender reveal was done by the child in the delivery room.

Lydia was named for the woman in Acts. The original Lydia was a businesswoman, believer, and hospitable to missionaries. The name Lydia is also said to derive from Greek and mean beautiful one or noble one.

> [13]On the Sabbath, we [Paul and his companions] went outside the city gate to the river, where we expected to find a place of prayer. We sat down and began to speak to the women who had gathered there. [14]One of those listening was a woman from the city of Thyatira named Lydia, a dealer in purple cloth. She was a worshiper of God. The Lord opened her heart to respond to Paul's message. [15]When she and the members of her household were baptized, she invited us to her home. "If you consider me a believer in the Lord," she said, "come and stay at my house." And she persuaded us.
>
> ACTS 16:13-15 (NIV)

Our Lydia's middle name is Faith which comes from Hebrews 11:1, "Now faith is the confidence in what we hope for and assurance about what we do not see." I had to first lay down the desire to have natural children before God was willing to grant her to me. My faith had to rest in trusting that if God wanted me to have natural children, He would bring it about in His timing. I will admit, there were times I struggled with having the faith that I would carry her to term successfully. I am believing that my Lydia will carry the positive character traits of Biblical Lydia and be a woman of even greater faith than me.

I heard many sermons growing up about the courageous Caleb. Caleb and Joshua were the men who went into the Promised Land and brought back good reports while the others did not.

> *They [the twelve spies] came back to Moses and Aaron and the whole Israelite community at Kadesh in the Desert of Paran. There they reported to them and to the whole assembly and showed them the fruit of the land. They gave Moses this account: "We went into the land to which you sent us, and it does flow with milk and honey! Here is its fruit. But the people who live there are powerful, and the cities are fortified and very large. We even saw descendants of Anak there. The Amalekites live in the Negev; the Hittites, Jebusites and Amorites live in the hill country; and the Canaanites live near the sea and along the Jordan." Then Caleb silenced the people before Moses and said, "We should go up and take possession of the land, for we can certainly do*

it." But the men who had gone up with him said, "We can't attack those people; they are stronger than we are." And they spread among the Israelites a bad report about the land they had explored. They said, "The land we explored devours those living in it. All the people we saw there are of great size. We saw the Nephilim there (the descendants of Anak come from the Nephilim). We seemed like grasshoppers in our own eyes, and we looked the same to them."

NUMBERS 13:26-30

Joshua son of Nun and Caleb son of Jephunneh, who were among those who had explored the land, tore their clothes and said to the entire Israelite assembly, "The land we passed through and explored is exceedingly good. If the Lord is pleased with us, he will lead us into that land, a land flowing with milk and honey, and will give it to us. Only do not rebel against the Lord. And do not be afraid of the people of the land, because we will devour them. Their protection is gone, but the Lord is with us. Do not be afraid of them."

NUMBERS 14:6-9

But because my servant Caleb has a different spirit and follows me wholeheartedly, I will bring him into the land he went to, and his descendants will inherit it.

NUMBERS 14:24

Of the men who went to explore the land, only Joshua
son of Nun and Caleb son of Jephunneh survived.

NUMBERS 14:38

I am believing that my Caleb will have that different spirit and be courageous, wholehearted, and faithful.

I never was partial to giving a child the exact name of their father, but variations of their father's name incorporated as a middle name, would be acceptable to me. Jose means may God add or give increase. God did add Caleb to the mix when I wasn't sure there would be another natural child, so Caleb caries Jose as his middle name.

Joshua means Jehovah is generous or Jehovah saves. It was Joshua and Caleb who went in to spy on the Promised Land along with the visionless other guys. It seemed only fitting to give Caleb his Biblical buddy. Once again, the middle name would come from his father, and Israel means may God prevail. I am believing that my Joshua will be generous and God will prevail in his life.

Nathaniel means gift of God, and in the Bible, Nathaniel was one of Jesus disciples.

Then Philip went to look for his friend, Nathanael, and
told him, "We've found him! We've found the One
we've been waiting for! It's Jesus, son of Joseph from
Nazareth, the Anointed One! He's the One that Moses
and the prophets prophesied would come!" Nathanael
sneered, "Nazareth! What good thing could ever come
from Nazareth?" Philip answered, "Come and let's find

out!" When Jesus saw Nathanael approaching, he said, "Now here comes a true son of Israel—an honest man with no hidden motive!" Nathanael was stunned and said, "But you've never met me—how do you know anything about me?" Jesus answered, "Nathanael, right before Philip came to you I saw you sitting under the shade of a fig tree." Nathanael blurted out, "Teacher, you are truly the Son of God and the King of Israel!" Jesus answered, "Do you believe simply because I told you I saw you sitting under a fig tree? You will experience even more impressive things than that! I prophesy to you eternal truth: From now on you will see an open heaven and gaze upon the Son of Man like a stairway reaching into the sky with the messengers of God climbing up and down upon him!"

JOHN 1:45-51, TPT

My prayer is that my Nathaniel will be an honest man, experience impressive things, and be spiritually perceptive. Joseph is the English version of Jose and also my brother's name. It means may God add or give increase. God had once again added to the family, so Joseph became his middle name.

Our natural name can speak to the destiny we are to pursue, but as we progress through life our choices and actions create a secondary name which has more to do with our character and what people associate with our name. The Bible speaks to the tremendous value of our character. "A good name is more desirable than great riches; to be esteemed is better than silver or gold" (Proverbs 22:1). May my children always pursue what is right and grow into fine men and women who are highly respected for great character.

Chapter 16
"You Are Not my Real Mom!"

———————————————————

I'm sure if I asked other adoptive mothers, many would say they heard the words, "You are not my real mom," uttered at least once in the heat of a battle with a teenager. I would hear those words from time to time come out of Mila's mouth and would retort back with, "Yes, and I didn't break you. I just have to try to help fix you. There, are we even?" I'm sure a psychologist would tell me that was not the proper way to handle the situation. Perhaps had I completed the psychology minor in college, I would have had a more appropriate response. I will say that no matter how poorly crafted my retort, it usually ended that little battle in a draw, and we could get back to whatever the real issue was at the time.

There was no denying that on some level, Mila's statement was accurate. I was not her real biological mom. My response to her statement of fact acknowledged that while that was true, it was not a complete representation of the situation. I had become her mom on two levels. First, I had become her mom in my heart, and second, I had become her mother in the eyes of the law through the legal adoption. While she did not always think of me as her mom, as far as I was concerned, she was my daughter. I would relentlessly fight and advocate for her when she could not. My role was to help her heal from the wounds she had experienced in those years before becoming my daughter and help guide her toward becoming a great woman.

When she arrived, her self-worth was low and goals were a foreign concept. By the time she left the nest, that same fiery fortitude with which she would fight me at times was being channeled to achieve success. She completed the Crucible at Parris Island to become a Marine.

The Marine Corp website explains: "The final challenge of recruit training is known as the Crucible. It is a 54-hour training exercise that validates the physical, mental and moral training they've endured throughout recruit training. The recruits are broken down into squads to face the challenges of the Crucible. They face challenges testing their physical strength, skills and the Marine Corps values they have learned throughout training. Throughout the event, the recruits are only allowed a limited amount of food and sleep. The final stage of the Crucible is a 9-mile hike from the training grounds to the Iwo Jima flag-raising statue at Peatross Parade Deck. Upon completing this challenge, the recruits are handed their Eagle, Globe and Anchors, symbolizing the completion of their arduous journey to become U.S. Marines."[1]

I may have had the fortitude to fight through the issues of parenting Mila, but I'm not sure I would survive the Crucible.

Perhaps if God had called me to the Marine Corps, He would have given me the strength to get through it. Instead, He called me to other things—including parenting her. People have said they don't know how I managed to get through life with her, and I think the only explanation can be God's grace.

The phrase, "You are not my real mom," can be difficult for the adoptive mom. It can feel like rejection. It can feel like being compared to someone who is on a pedestal yet isn't in the picture and making the hard decisions of parenting. Because our children were adopted from within the extended family, this would realistically have to be an open adoption. I knew at some point, their biological mom might come back into their lives. On some level, I feared that day wondering if I would be rejected even after how much of my heart I had invested in them. Once they were both legal adults, their biological mother reached out to them via social media. It was easy to have lots of grace for their mom during the adoption process because it was a one-way extending of grace. If she now became involved in their lives could I continue to be gracious or would some territorial competitive attitude rise up? Would she approve of the job I had done parenting her biological children?

I will never forget the night she came to our house for the first time after reconnecting with Mila and Navo. If I could have scripted the meeting, my house would have been in perfect order and I would have been dressed well with the hair and makeup perfect. I would have looked like I had everything together and was living up to some superhuman standard. Maybe it was just to give me a grandiose slice of humble pie that God decided to mess up my ideal situation. I was out at a job site wrapping up a large event for our family business when I received the call that she was going to be arriving at the house at about the same time that I would be pulling into the driveway. I would not be the image of perfection. My hair would be in whatever disheveled mess from wind and working. My makeup would be whatever was left from early that morning. I would be in jeans and a uniform shirt that showed I had been doing physical work. I might be a random mix of smells of snack foods and sweat. Obviously, whatever condition my house was in when I left earlier that day would be what she would see. There was no time to make it magazine photo shoot ready.

It was sort of awkward but nothing monumentally disastrous. Their biological mother was doing well. Our children now had another half-sibling, and the little sister they remembered was becoming a young woman.

I do not need to be jealous of my children's relationship with their biological mom. There is room for both of us in their lives. She gave them life and I have given them a life. Their relationship with her today is much more like adult friends, while I retain more of the parent/adult child relationship.

My children obviously knew they were adopted and knew their biological parents. I once learned of an adult around my age suddenly learning he had to have been adopted because an ancestry DNA test revealed there was no way he was biologically related to the siblings he had always known. His parents had taken this information to their graves. He was wrestling with whether to find out the details of his birth. After 40 years of living, would finding out those details help him or hinder him? Would those facts reframe his self-worth in a positive or negative way? While they may identify something of his start in life, they had not consciously and actively impacted who he had become up to this point. I cannot honestly say if put in that position whether I would want to find out the details about my birth or not. While I have no idea what it would truly feel like to be in that position, I can completely understand that it could significantly shake up a person's world for a season.

Knowing the facts surrounding circumstances of conception, identities of biological parents, or reasons for choosing adoption can cloud correct perception of self-worth even though it should not. Because of the nature of our children's adoption, we know many of the facts and they know them also. No matter what the facts are, there is truth that supersedes all of those facts. My children, any adopted child, and for that matter, any natural born child can find their identity in the truth of God's word.

Truth says you are made in the image of God. "So God created mankind in his own image, in the image of God he created them; male and female he created them" (Genesis 1:27). He is the all-knowing Creator of the universe with the capacity to love without limit. He created us with the capacity for great intelligence and to love like He does. While we may display physical characteristics similar to our biological parents, we were still created in His supreme image.

Truth says God put you together in the womb and you are wonderfully made. Even if something in your design seems flawed in the eyes of human standards, you are not flawed in God's eyes. He is perfect and does not make mistakes.

> *"For you created my inmost being; you knit me together*
> *in my mother's womb. I praise you because I am fearfully*

and wonderfully made; your works are wonderful, I know that full well. My frame was not hidden from you when I was made in the secret place, when I was woven together in the depths of the earth. Your eyes saw my unformed body; all the days ordained for me were written in your book before one of them came to be.

PSALM 139:13-16

Truth says God has a plan for you.

Before I formed you in the womb I knew you, before you were born I set you apart.

JEREMIAH 1:5a, NIV

"For I know the plans I have for you," declares the Lord, "plans to prosper you and not to harm you, plans to give you hope and a future."

JEREMIAH 29:11

Our future and God's plan are not defined by or limited by our biological parents or adoptive parents. Truth says you were created to do great things.

For we are God's handiwork, created in Christ Jesus to do good works, which God prepared in advance for us to do.

EPHESIANS 2:10

Very truly I tell you, whoever believes in me will do the works I have been doing, and they will do even greater things than these, because I am going to the Father.

JOHN 14:12

Truth says even our mistakes do not condemn us to a life outside His plan.

> *Therefore, there is now no condemnation for those who are in Christ Jesus, because through Christ Jesus the law of the Spirit who gives life has set you free from the law of sin and death.*
>
> ROMANS 8:1

When we've accepted Christ, we are no longer condemned. We are set free to be all God designed us to be. Truth says God wants good to come from even the messiest of situations.

> *And we know that in all things God works for the good of those who love him, who have been called according to his purpose.*
>
> ROMANS 8:28

My adopted children may have had a messy start in life but God has worked through that mess to bring about good things. While I wouldn't say that my three miscarriages were good, I do know that God has used those experiences to make me better.

Truth says God has our back and will take care of us.

> *If God is for us, who can be against us? He who did not spare his own Son, but gave him up for us all—how will he not also, along with him, graciously give us all things?*
>
> ROMANS 8:31b-32

Truth says we are designed to be more than conquerors and nothing can separate us from God's love—even our mess ups and failures.

> *Now, in all these things we are more than conquerors through him who loved us. For I am convinced that neither death nor life, neither angels nor demons, neither the present nor the future, nor any powers, neither height nor depth, nor anything else in all creation, will be able to separate us from the love of God that is in Christ Jesus our Lord.*
>
> ROMANS 8:37-39

Truth says obedience brings blessings.

> *All these blessings will come on you and accompany you if you obey the LORD your God: You will be blessed in the city and blessed in the country. The fruit of your womb will be blessed, and the crops of your land and the young of your livestock—the calves of your herds and the lambs of your flocks. Your basket and your kneading trough will be blessed. You will be blessed when you come in and blessed when you go out. The LORD will grant that the enemies who rise up against you will be defeated before you. They will come at you from one direction but flee from you in seven. The LORD will send a blessing on your barns and on everything you put your hand to. The LORD your God will bless you in the land he is giving you ... The LORD will grant you abundant*

prosperity—in the fruit of your womb, the young of your livestock and the crops of your ground—in the land he swore to your ancestors to give you. The LORD will open the heavens, the storehouse of his bounty, to send rain on your land in season and to bless all the work of your hands. You will lend to many nations but will borrow from none. The LORD will make you the head, not the tail. If you pay attention to the commands of the LORD your God that I give you this day and carefully follow them, you will always be at the top, never at the bottom.

DEUTERONOMY 28:2-8, 11-13

Truth says we can be content in our circumstances, and He will give us the strength to be so.

I am not saying this because I am in need, for I have learned to be content whatever the circumstances. I know what it is to be in need, and I know what it is to have plenty. I have learned the secret of being content in any and every situation, whether well fed or hungry, whether living in plenty or in want. I can do all this through him who gives me strength.

PHILIPPIANS 4:11-13

Facts about your biological roots don't change your worth, your value, your destiny, etc. Even though humans can fail us, God won't. He loves us so much that he sent His son to die on our behalf and pay the price for our sins that separate us from Him. Nothing we can do on our own can make us acceptable to God.

For the wages of sin is death, but the gift of God is eternal life in Christ Jesus our Lord.

ROMANS 6:23, NIV

For it is by grace you have been saved, through faith— and this is not from yourselves, it is the gift of God— not by works, so that no one can boast.

EPHESIANS 2:8-9, NIV

This righteousness is given through faith in Jesus Christ to all who believe. There is no difference between Jew and Gentile, for all have sinned and fall short of the glory of God, and all are justified freely by his grace through the redemption that came by Christ Jesus.

ROMANS 3:22-34, NIV

You see, at just the right time, when we were still powerless, Christ died for the ungodly. Very rarely will anyone die for a righteous person, though for a good person someone might possibly dare to die. But God demonstrates his own love for us in this: While we were still sinners, Christ died for us.

ROMANS 5:6-8, NIV

Jesus is the supreme advocate to the Father.

"I tell you, my friends, do not be afraid of those who kill the body and after that can do no more. But I will show you whom you should fear: Fear him who, after

your body has been killed, has authority to throw you into hell. Yes, I tell you, fear him. Are not five sparrows sold for two pennies? Yet not one of them is forgotten by God. Indeed, the very hairs of your head are all numbered. Don't be afraid; you are worth more than many sparrows. "I tell you, whoever publicly acknowledges me before others, the Son of Man will also acknowledge before the angels of God.

LUKE 12:4-8, NIV

If you've never had your identity framed by becoming a child of God, the ultimate parent, you can accept the free offer of salvation through His Son. You are then adopted into His family, and He's the best daddy there is. You can then boast in a daddy who created the entire universe and still cares about every hair on your head. Through your position as His child, you have access to everything He has, including all of His armor for any battle you face.

Just as Mila had to consent to her adoption into our family, we each must consent to adoption into God's family. He gave each of us a free will, and as much as He wants us in His family, He won't force us into His family. A simple conversation with him brings us into His family.

Dear Jesus, I know I am a sinner. I believe You died on the cross for my sins. Right now, I turn from my sins and open my heart and life to You and accept You as my personal Savior. Thank you Jesus for saving me.

If you just prayed that prayer there is an adoption party happening in heaven. Now, read *New to Jesus?* (page 205).

"That's the way God responds every time one lost sinner repents and turns to Him. He says to all His angels, 'Let's have a joyous celebration, for that one who was lost I have found!'"

LUKE 15:10, TPT

You also become Jesus' brother or sister.

"Anyone who does the will of my Father in heaven is my brother and sister and mother!"

MATTHEW 12:50, NLT

You also are joint heirs with him.

"And you did not receive the 'spirit of religious duty,' leading you back into the fear of never being good enough. But you have received the 'Spirit of full acceptance,' enfolding you into the family of God. And you will never feel orphaned, for as he rises up within us, our spirits join him in saying the words of tender affection, 'Beloved Father!' For the Holy Spirit makes God's fatherhood real to us as he whispers into our innermost being, 'You are God's beloved child!' And since we are his true children, we qualify to share all his treasures, for indeed, we are heirs of God himself. And since we are joined to Christ, we also inherit all that he is and all that he has."

ROMANS 8:15-17a, TPT

ENDNOTE

1. https://www.mcrdpi.marines.mil/Recruit-Training/Crucible/.

Chapter 17
How Many Children
do You Have?

Children are God's love-gift; they are heaven's generous
reward. Children born to a young couple will one day
rise to protect and provide for their parents. Happy
will be the couple who has many of them! A household
full of children will not bring shame on your name but
victory when you face your enemies, for your offspring
will have influence and honor to prevail on your behalf!

PSALM 127:3-5, THE PASSION TRANSLATION

It is not uncommon in everyday conversation for the question, "How many children do you have?" to be asked. A non-traditional response tends to roll off my tongue. "It depends on how you want to count them." That at times opens up an interesting conversation. I often say you could get to ten—one step, two adopted, three natural in heaven, four natural on earth.

From there, I may clarify how many I have had to actively parent or state the number that I have to keep track of daily to avoid being in an unflattering story on the front page of the newspaper.

When answering the question of how many children you have, I believe there are endless combinations of possibilities. In my own life, the following possibilities have been present at one time or another … a step child, kinship foster children, adopted children, natural children in heaven, natural children on earth, sponsored children, etc.

You could answer it based on children you are legally responsible for at the moment. You could answer it based on children who have ever been within your care. You could answer it based on those you've emotionally attached to or with whom you are in an active parenting or mentoring role. Having children is so much more than passing on genetic material to a new life. Passing on genetic material doesn't have to be the prerequisite to having children.

HAVING CHILDREN IS SO MUCH MORE THAN PASSING ON GENETIC MATERIAL TO A NEW LIFE

Do you have a child if you are a full-time parent to a stepchild and identify with that child as your own because you are emotionally attached and actively engaged? I would argue, yes, you have a child. What if you are only a part-time parent, but are still emotionally attached and actively engaged in the life of the stepchild? Again, I would argue you have a child. What if you are a legal stepparent who wants to emotionally attach and actively engage but doesn't have the opportunity to do so? I would argue you get more credit for being a parent than does the person who actively chooses not to emotionally attach and actively engage. I believe parenting comes down to a choice and attitude of your heart.

I have known couples who have not had children living with them in their home but were stand-in parents to nieces and nephews, and in some cases, footing the bill for college educations. There are coaches, teachers, scout leaders, and pastors who have stepped up to be a parental role model for children in other families or for seasons for children in broken or problem-ridden families. Some people sponsor children overseas through organizations like Compassion and World Vision who are immensely active in writing letters and praying for their sponsor children.

If you aren't sure how many children you have, you may just need to take a look around. Whose faces are in pictures on your walls or on your desk? Whose pictures may be scrolling on your computer screen saver? In all likelihood, those pictures display those people who are most important in your life. I know for me, my office screen saver scrolls the assorted collection of adopted, natural, and sponsored children. With my adopted and natural children, I have played a very active role while with my sponsored children, it is a much different kind of activity.

In identifying your children, I could also ask who are you praying for regularly? Perhaps you are a spiritual mom or dad for someone. Perhaps you are fighting on your knees for someone else's child as if he or she is your own.

"Be fruitful and multiply" is often quoted from the Bible with the connotation that is all about bringing new children into the world. Being fruitful and multiplying is so much more than that. There is something to be said for those who are being "fruitful" by taking children who are already here and choosing to "multiply" by training them up in the way they should go and actively investing in them to help them become all God designed them to be.

Sadly, there are parents who lose children and that does not change that they were a parent, even if only for a short time. I remember one time standing with a woman who had just miscarried yet another baby. She was crushed. She had battled infertility for years, and while technically she had only been pregnant a very short time, she had emotionally attached to that child who was very much wanted. To say she was not a mother would invalidate the existence of that child she dearly loved. She will always be a mother, it's just her child is in heaven.

When I lost my first baby, my husband and I along with several family members attended the Share Burial, a common burial for miscarriage, stillborn, and early loss infants. I hadn't personally known other women who had been through a miscarriage, and on some level, it was comforting to look around and see other grieving mothers and realize I was not alone. Having that funeral and a place to go back to if I wanted, helped validate the existence of my child and put closure to the loss.

After the loss of my second baby, I debated on whether to go to the Share burial. I knew I would be going alone, but that was okay. At the last minute, I decided I would take a break from work and head over. I was there by myself and stood off to the side. Another woman approached me and asked if I was there for my child. We ended up sharing our stories. She too was burying a daughter. We shared how God had touched each of us in uniquely special ways to say our children were in heaven and things would be okay. She remembered my name and a few months later, I received a Mother's Day card from her. It was so touching. Even in her own loss, she was validating that I too was a mother of natural children, they just weren't with me.

She started a women's group, and for a season I would go hang out at her house once a month. Finally, one month I pulled her aside after the group and let her know I was again expecting. I knew I likely wouldn't be able to hide it the next time I saw her and wanted to give her time to adjust to the news since she too had lost babies, and I knew how much seeing a pregnant woman could be a trigger. I was always happy for women who I knew had struggled, but there was a part of me that was jealous when I was still waiting. By the next time I saw her, she was ready to tell me that she too was expecting. Both of us successfully carried our children to term.

If you have never had the opportunity to parent a child in your home, please do not feel devalued as a man or a woman. God still has plans and a calling on your life and it could be something even greater than could be done with just one or two children in your home. He may be using you to impact an even larger population of children. He doesn't forget the desires of your heart and may bring about something even better than you ever dreamed possible. He doesn't show us the bigger picture all at once because we would likely try to rush it and mess it up. We simply have to

GOD STILL HAS PLANS AND A CALLING ON YOUR LIFE AND IT COULD BE SOMETHING EVEN GREATER trust Him through each and every step, even though I fully admit that's not always the easiest thing to do. You may find in eternity that you have more "children" than you realize. I know there are people I've looked up to as a parent-like role models who have significantly impacted my life even if only from a distance.

Chapter 18
Silly Polo Ball

The warrior spirit was strong in me during the fight for Mila's mental and emotional healing. A seemingly random accident on a Sunday afternoon brought me back to that place and I felt the warrior spirit rise up again from its fifteen or so years of dormancy. This time the warrior spirit was on behalf of a natural child.

It was a typical Sunday afternoon in August 2017. We went to the local polo game like we had done so many times for several years. The game started off like any other game. The ball was tossed into the group of eight ponies and riders. They raced back and forth up and down the field trying to get that hard little ball between the two upright posts at the end of the field. Each time they scored, they would switch directions and pursue the goal at the opposite end so as not to give either team an advantage or disadvantage. There were young players and older players. It's generally not an overly competitive game for this group. At times players switch teams to keep things balanced or to give someone a break.

For those on the sideline, it's a great time of tailgating. Some people bring nice spreads of fine cheese, hors d'oeuvres, and wine. Others, like us, bring child-friendly things like Colby jack, Doritos, Oreos, and Gatorade. It's generally a pleasurable and relaxing time hanging out on a Sunday afternoon with friends, watching a game, and enjoying the outdoors. In between chuckers, the children can go out on the field and stomp divots or toss footballs, Frisbees, or softballs. It's also possible to engage in a mini-game of polo with short practice mallets.

Polo balls are quite hard and can fly quickly. Very rarely does one go out of bounds. In fact, it's been more common for me to see a horse step out of bounds closer to the spectators than for a ball to come out. This particular Sunday, in a freak accident, a ball came flying our direction. It whizzed past everyone in front of the tree line but as Joshua was turning it struck him on the cheek. He let out an ear-piercing scream that could be heard on the other side of the field. He was just six years old. I ran to him and wrapped my arms around him. The sidelines were filled with tail gaiters which meant there was lots of ice around, so within moments we had a bag of ice on his face. Play stopped, and the announcer asked for any nurses or doctors in the crowd to go over to that area of the sidelines. He requested someone to signal whether they should call for an ambulance.

I wish I could say I was the epitome of strength and faith in that instant but I wasn't. All I could muster was, "Joshua, you are going to be okay," as he screamed in pain. I was very overwhelmed and thoughts were flying all around my head. I found myself falling back on truth I had learned in church as a child and began praying in the Spirit over him. My mind got the reset it needed and that faith-filled warrior spirit rose up. My child was going to come through this, and God was going to get the glory.

I FOUND MYSELF FALLING BACK ON TRUTH I HAD LEARNED IN CHURCH AS A CHILD.

A doctor and nurse came over and they felt pretty confident that this was not a catastrophic injury. A tall gentleman in a royal blue shirt came over and stood just to my left. I noticed he was wearing a cross, so I was pretty sure I knew why he was there. In fact, he did pray over us before we left in the ambulance. Interestingly, this gentleman fell into that pattern I've seen elsewhere in my life when God chooses to use a human to deliver a message that He wants to bypass my brain and go directly into my heart. Once again, this was a tall man, again probably a subconscious symbol of power and authority. He was a complete stranger and my memory was blocked from retaining anything that I could use to identify him later. I believe God didn't want me to disqualify the message using my intellect or to associate the message with a specific individual. Some might suggest it was an angel, but I still subscribe to the belief that they are humans who are being obedient when God tells them to do or say something. In this case, the message I was getting was that God was still in control, Joshua was going to be fine, and this was to be bigger than just about us.

I rode with Joshua in the ambulance to the hospital while the rest of the family followed in the minivan. I had patient number one to attend to, but knew I would need to attend to the other children soon. They had just witnessed a very scary event and would need help processing it all.

By nothing less than the grace of God and the protective hands of angels, Joshua walked out of the hospital in a few hours with the report of nothing broken. He'd have a mark for a few days but no permanent damage. I hearken back to the discussion on names. Joshua means Jehovah is generous or Jehovah saves. Israel means God prevails. God did prevail and was generous in saving Joshua from what could have been a very bad situation.

Romans 8:28 says, "We know that all things work together for good to them that love God, to them who are the called according to his purpose." The verse doesn't say all things **are good** but it says all things **work together for good**. Of course, the good doesn't necessarily happen on its own or by accident. The good may require some obedience along the way. Luke 12:48 says, "From everyone who has been given much, much will be demanded; and from the one who has been entrusted with much, much more will be asked." When we got home, I knew I now had responsibilities to fulfill.

I had just been given a miracle that my child walked away basically unscathed from an accident that could have been catastrophic. That ball had grazed and ricocheted off his cheek. It had missed his mouth, his nose, his eyes, his ears, and the entire area of his brain.

First, I would need to report to everyone that Joshua was going to be okay. Facebook, I will gladly use you to declare the goodness of God. Here is what I posted:

Today, Joshua's face and a polo ball had an unfriendly interaction in a completely freak accident. The ball didn't know it was messing with a child of God. The Great Physician was already at work when the friendly nurse and doctor stepped forward from among the fans to check on him. The EMTs were great, and Joshua was a brave and calm patient for them in his first ever ambulance ride. He got to get a CT scan in the cool "donut" machine and was well cared for by the hospital team. The medical professionals were able to deliver the good report ... no broken bones.

"The righteous person may have many troubles, but the Lord delivers him from them all; he protects all his bones, not one of them will be broken."

PSALM 34:19-20

I wish I could say I used all my biblical scholarly wisdom and just pulled that verse about no bones being broken out of my head, but that would be lying. The reality is there must have been divine assistance in my internet searching and that verse came up. I shared the verse with my little crew and they had one of those "Wow, that's cool" moments. They now had a tangible experience of the truth of God's word and in this particular instance God chose to protect all of Joshua's bones. These teaching moments are great but they aren't necessarily easy and do require intentionality.

My second responsibility was to reach out to the coach of the young players who were out on the field that day. I had no idea who happened to have hit the ball and it didn't really matter to me. There were no hard feelings. It was purely an accident. I was concerned that this event might plant a seed of fear or doubt in the hearts of the young players. The young players were there through a special program that gives at-risk youth a chance to work with the horses in exchange for the opportunity to learn about and play polo. It's an extremely successful program and has opened tremendous doors for many young people. If polo is part of God's plan and purpose for those young people, the last thing I would want is for them to walk away from the sport because they saw a child get a minor injury.

"WHY ME?" IS A NATURAL QUESTION WHEN SOMETHING BAD HAPPENS

My third responsibility was to walk Joshua through processing what happened. One of the natural questions that comes up when something bad happens is, "Why me?" I have asked God that question many times. He often chooses not to give me a straight answer and, quite frankly, it is probably because He knows that deep down inside I already know the answer. It is a fallen world, so sometimes bad things happen and if I cooperate He can still use the bad things for good. In Joshua's case, he was very much looking to me for an answer to his "Why me?" How does one spin a story for a six-year-old who's been hit in the face with a polo ball that God was in any way, shape, or form looking out for him. As I spun the story, there had to be some divine creativity coming through.

"Joshua, let me explain what happened. Sunday morning God called all of the angels together for their normal morning staff meeting where He tells them what their assignments are for the day. God told two of the angels to stick around after the meeting because they had a special assignment. 'Okay guys, today you are going to the polo match and you are in charge of Joshua. There's going to be an accident and a polo ball is going to come out of bounds headed for him. Your job is to protect all of the important parts of his head and just kind of let the ball skid off of his check. I want some drama, but not too much drama. Do you think you can handle that?' 'Got it,' they responded. Then the angels made their plan. 'I'll do this,' (now imagine a mom pretending to be an angel doing some serious overacting and putting her hands all over Joshua's face) and 'I'll do this' (more moving the hands around to cover eyes, nose, mouth, etc.)."

Naturally, the result was a six-year-old laughing at how silly mommy was, but he was getting the spiritual truth that God had it all under control and his guardian angels were at work.

God continued to use that little incident throughout the week. At work, a gentleman from a vendor overheard me talking and joined the conversation. He had dealt with being in the hospital with a child but his was the case of a failed suicide attempt. God laid very specific things on my heart to share with him and his daughter. I may never know this side of heaven what impact my obedience had. All I am called to do is share when told to share. God is the one who does the rest.

As the next Sunday rolled around, I felt a strong urge to be prepared. I didn't know what that might look like, but my radar was up for opportunities. I knew we had to go to the polo match, and didn't want fear to creep into Joshua's little spirit. I wanted to be there in person to show he was fine and there were no hard feelings.

As we were heading to the field, I asked Joshua if he found out who happened to have hit the ball that hit him whether he could forgive that person. His first response was a rather definite "No, he hurt me." I asked him if it was intentional. He retorted, "Yes." Once again, mom was going to have to come up with a divinely inspired creative spin.

"Joshua, you've seen how many times they aim for that big space between the uprights to make a goal and can't get the ball through. Do you really think they are that good that they can aim for and hit a little boy who moves around as much as you?" He had to admit that I had a point.

In my second asking of the question of whether or not this was intentional Joshua replied, "No," and shook his head, grasping that the player had not tried to hit him on purpose.

I then asked Joshua if we happened to learn who hit the ball could he give the player a hug. Forgiveness and grace can be tough concepts for a child to wrap their head around, but if they can give a hug that's a pretty good indicator of the condition of their heart. He wasn't yet ready to commit on that one but at least the seed had been planted.

When we arrived at the field, we headed directly to the announcer's booth. I was on a mission. I wanted them to know that Joshua was back and they could see he was fine. The player who hit the ball heard the announcer mention that Joshua was over by the booth. He rode over to apologize and dismounted from the horse. Standing before us was one of the young players and this happened to be his seventeenth birthday. Without even a moment of hesitation, Joshua hugged him. The announcer continued the play-by-play so that everyone at the field that day, even if they couldn't see it, could hear that Joshua was hugging the polo player. He then handed me the microphone and I was able to thank the people who were there for us and to share some of the great things that God had done using a silly little polo ball accident.

I'm so glad I had been obedient to the nudge of the Holy Spirit to be prepared and had my radar up.

> *"Therefore, as God's chosen people, holy and dearly loved, clothe yourselves with compassion, kindness, humility, gentleness and patience. Bear with each other and forgive one another if any of you has a grievance against someone. Forgive as the Lord forgave you. And over all these virtues put on love, which binds them all together in perfect unity."*
>
> COLOSSIANS 3:12-14

Over the rest of the season, Joshua would intentionally go seek out that player to say hello. Forgiveness and love really do bind people together in unity.

Good parenting isn't for the faint of heart, but God will give you guidance as you go if you are open to it. Sometimes, it's the loud stuff like, "Are you sure this is my will" and other times it's the quiet little nudges that feel more like following your gut instinct.

In some ways, that silly polo ball is responsible for this book. As I was drifting off to sleep the night of the accident I couldn't help but reflect over the events of the day. I thought through my own actions and reactions in the heat of the moment. I realized that when my natural mind had reached the end of what it could do mustering up the marginally faith-filled, "Joshua, you are going to be okay," it shut down and my spirit took over. While I prayed in the Spirit, my natural mind got a reboot. I had fallen back on something I had learned when I was not that much older than Joshua. It became apparent to me that I would need to seek out a new church where my children would be exposed to the type of teaching I received as a child. I found that church, and it was there that I attended the writer's conference that spurred me on to write this book. Thank you silly little polo ball!

Chapter 19
Heroes and Generational Blessings

I believe it is safe to say we've all had heroes in our life at one point or another. As children we may have said, "I want to be like so and so." As we learned the difference between cartoons and reality, we may have discovered that "so and so" wasn't even real. As we shifted to this world of reality, our heroes may have been found around our family such as an older sibling, a parent, grandparent, aunt, uncle, etc. Our heroes may also have come in our larger network at school, at church, or in the wider community where we live. It's also possible we have considered someone in the public eye to be our hero because of some special skill. The person could be an amazing gymnast, basketball player, artist, musician, singer, or whatever. As we mature, we hopefully look to heroes for things of real significance and greater substance. Character and attitude will likely exist long beyond the special talents or abilities of our heroes.

The more removed a hero is from our daily lives, the easier it can be to put them on a pedestal. We can easily be tempted to think their life is perfect, but that's likely not true. We may think they have it all together but that's not necessarily true either. Just because they excel in one thing doesn't mean they excel in everything. If we really stop to think about it, there is probably just one or two things about the person which really stand out and impress us. If we could create the perfect version of ourself, or at least what we would perceive to be the perfect version, we would likely try to incorporate all of those best qualities from a whole lot of people into that one perfect version. While it may seem admirable to try to exemplify all of those best qualities, it is also incredibly unrealistic.

In Ephesians 5, we are commanded to be like Christ. With that as our highest goal, I would postulate that many of those most admirable qualities I have seen in others are the qualities of Christ that they have mastered or where they have seemingly outperformed the average. For all of those wonderful qualities they exemplify, I would be willing to bet there was considerable learning and lots of mistakes along the way. It is equally likely that they experienced considerable challenges, obstacles, and heartache as they navigated their way to "success." The success is what most of us see and not the long backstory that they traveled to that point. It is the backstory where character development likely occurred and very few get to shortcut to "success." If there was a shortcut and they are in the public eye, sadly, they will likely be brutally demonized if they fail rather than be given the grace to allow them to get back up again.

As I think over my life, I've often admired successful business people who have used their business platform for greater things. It's not so much their monetary success I've learned to admire but the character with which they have handled that success.

Dave Thomas, the founder of Wendy's, has always been way up there on my hero list. He was born to a young unmarried woman and adopted as a baby. He learned the value of hard work and determination and built a tremendously successful business. He never forgot his roots, and through his success, was able to give back.

As a teenager, I had the opportunity to attend a national convention for Junior Achievement where he was to be one of the keynote speakers. I was looking forward to seeing him. Everyone knew Wendy's, especially from the long running "Where's the Beef?" commercials. It was not uncommon for our family to stop at a Wendy's for burgers and Frosties. Dave had started appearing in the commercials and came across like a genuine person who was worth emulating. He had one of those rags to riches stories that would resonate with many of the junior achievement young people from around the country who were all gathered there in Indiana. Unfortunately, medical issues forced him to cancel that appearance and one of the gentleman who worked for him came instead.

> *Dave believed that everyone has a responsibility to give something back to the community. The cause closest to his heart was adoption. Adopted as an infant, Dave felt a strong personal tie to those children who were waiting to be adopted. He said he was lucky to have been adopted and wanted every waiting child to have a permanent home and loving family.*

In 1990, President Bush asked Dave to head the White House Initiative on Adoption. With his background as an adoptee and his stature in the business community, he accepted the challenge of raising awareness for the cause. Dave found that there were several obstacles to adoption: the red tape and paperwork was usually overwhelming, and the process too expensive for prospective parents. There were families in America who wanted to adopt, but the obstacles were often too great.

With this focus, Dave set his course. He devoted time and energy to special adoption programs, including a letter-writing campaign to Fortune 1000 CEOs asking them to make adoption benefits available to their employees. He also met with U.S. Governors and asked them to offer adoption benefits to state employees.
In 1992, he established the Dave Thomas Foundation for Adoption, a not-for-profit organization that provides grants to national and regional adoption organizations for programs that raise awareness and make adoption easier and more affordable.

He realized many successes in his work for the cause. In 1996 President Clinton signed the Tax Credit Bill into law that gives adoptive parents a one-time tax credit of $5,000 when they adopt. And in 1997, President Clinton signed the Adoption and Safe FamiliesAct, which reduces waiting time for children in foster care, speeds up the adoption process and has built-in accountability and state incentives.[1]

Dave Thomas' book, *Dave's Way*, came out during my college years and I quickly read it. I'm glad I had heroes like him when I started college. While I definitely felt the allure of power, prestige, and wealth surrounding me in college, there was a piece of me that was already grounded in knowing there's more to life than those things. Business success is something to be stewarded for the greater good. Dave stewarded it toward adoption, and while I never met him face to face, he impacted the formation of my family. His work in Washington helped bring about the tax credit which helped our family cover the cost of the attorney fees necessary to finalize Mila and Navo's adoption. Thank you, Dave!

Closer to home, Anne Beiler, founder of Auntie Anne's Soft Pretzels has made my hero list. She's from the same area of Pennsylvania and became a blessed business owner. I admire her business success and her amazing giving heart.

As I was finishing up this book, I had the opportunity to hear Anne speak at a Mother's Day church service. Joshua was quite interested in her books and thus I bought her newest book, *The Secret Lies Within – An Inside Out Look at Overcoming Trauma and Finding Purpose in the Pain,* and her other book, *Twist of Faith.* As I read through the books, my "hero" became more of a "real person." She tragically lost a child. She went through trials and trauma. She experienced deep valleys of pain as well as the mountain top experiences in the public eye of which I was much more familiar. She allowed God to use the bad things to make good things come. Yes, she experienced pain but it was through the pain that she and Jonas found purpose. In *Twist of Faith* she says, "Our purpose would be to give financially to people and ministries in need," which they have gone on to do. The passion to provide counseling for other couples put Anne and Jonas on the path toward the pretzel. She goes on to say, "I know that Auntie Anne's was about far more than pretzels, money, or success. The franchise was born out of a story of redemption that needed to be shared. Only through the unexpected success of

Auntie's Anne's could I speak in front of large audiences and share my story on national television. God gave me a pretzel, then He gave me a platform." Only God could orchestrate the amazing journey she has taken from humble beginnings and challenges to the heights of success and the opportunity to positively influence and speak into the lives of so many.

I've been a part of two small businesses to date but neither one has catapulted me to the level of success of Dave Thomas or Anne Beiler. One day, I was sort of arguing with God about it. Why can't I be like Anne? Of course, knowing more about the road she's walked I don't think I realized what I would have been asking for. I felt Him say, "Maybe that's not what I have for you." I was then challenged to look at someone who was likely very influential in her life. It was her mother. Amanda attended the same church as me, and I had a few occasions to speak with her. She was a humble and sweet woman. After she passed away I read her obituary and it spoke volumes.

> *Amanda Glick Smucker passed away peacefully just after midnight on Tuesday, October 16th (2012) at 92 years of age. It was a cold autumn night and the stars shone brightly. For the last week of her life on earth she was surrounded by the love, laughter, and prayers of her family. If you would have passed by the house, you would have heard them singing. It sounded like heaven. Amanda entered this world on July 29, 1920, born to Jacob R. and Annie Stoltzfus Glick on Geist Road in Leola, PA. She married Eli Smucker in November of 1941.*

> *Their grandson Brandon Smucker recently noted that from her children and grandchildren came "pastors, teachers, writers, missionaries, counselors, photographers, homemakers, quilters, nurses, videographers,*

musicians, business leaders, athletes, entrepreneurs, and motivational speakers. So many world changers from one woman."

Amanda and Eli remained married until his passing on January 29th, 1983. From that time on she made a living as a quilter, running her own quilt shop for over 25 years. She personally presented a quilt to President Ronald Reagan in 1988 and sent quilts to numerous Presidents after that. Her life was a living representation of the "woman of valor" in Proverbs 31 (vs 27-31) She watches over the affairs of her household and does not eat the bread of idleness. Her children arise and call her blessed; her husband also, and he praises her: "Many women do noble things, but you surpass them all." Charm is deceptive, and beauty is fleeting; but a woman who fears the LORD is to be praised. Honor her for all that her hands have done, and let her works bring her praise at the city gate.[2]

The words jumped out at me. "So many world changers from one woman." While I call Anne a hero for what she's been able to do in the public eye, I could just as equally call her mother, Amanda, a hero for rearing children who have excelled in their God-given gifts and talents. She may not have gotten everything right all of the time, but there's no denying she did something right. Her children have built on the foundation she laid. It's also very likely Amanda built on a foundation laid in her from the generation before.

Some people talk a lot about generational curses, but I think there is something even greater in generational blessings. I really like how Ricardo White explained the concept in his book, *The Anchor*, "You can leave your children money, but when you leave them a godly heritage, when you model a life of excellence, that's worth more than any material thing that you could ever leave them. God's blessing on our lives will cause us to go farther than if we had all the money in the world. You can have few resources, but with generational blessings nothing will be impossible for you."

Anne started with few resources but built an international business. I think it's safe to say she may have benefited from some generational blessings both on her side of the family and that of her husband. In *Twist of Faith*, she spoke of how Jonas' formative years had challenges and he ended up helping his aunts in the kitchen. His early experience with baking opened the door for the development of their secret recipe. As they were looking to buy their first stand, it was Jonas' father who helped them with a loan. Each generation invests in the next generation in one way or another. Hopefully, the investments are in good things like character, talents, vision, etc. Just as pain can bring purpose within a life, pain across generations can bring purpose for future generations. God allowed the child of a young unmarried woman to found Wendy's, so while there was likely pain in her pregnancy and her choice to put her child up for adoption, and perhaps pain in unanswered questions for Dave, God allowed it to be part of a greater purpose to find loving homes for so many more children and renewed hope for future generations.

I've been the recipient of generational blessings from the strong heritage of faith and service that came down through my great grandparents and grandmother. With those blessings also comes responsibility. "From everyone who has been given much, much will be demanded; and from the one who has been entrusted with much, much more will be asked" (Luke 12:48b). I must sow seeds into the next generation to continue the generational blessings. "The benevolent man leaves an inheritance that endures to his children's children" (Proverbs 13:22).

In *The Anchor,* Ricardo went on to say, "God always shows us farther than we can go. You may have a dream or a vision that may not be accomplished in your lifetime – that's a generational vision." I have to admit I don't think I had ever actually thought of visions going across generations even though there is an example sitting right there in the Bible. Abraham was told, "I will surely bless you and make your descendants as numerous as the stars in the sky and as the sand on the seashore. Your descendants will take possession of the cities of their enemies, and through your offspring all nations on earth will be blessed, because you have obeyed me" (Genesis 22:17-18, NIV). Obviously that was a generational vision and promise that he would not live to see while here on the earth.

Maybe I'm not "Anne" but rather "Amanda." Maybe I'm not destined to have the hugely successful business, but rather to be the generation that lays a foundation for future generations to step into their callings. Maybe I'm sowing the seeds and there is an "Anne" among the harvest of my descendants. Maybe the generational heritage of faith, serving and giving will see an exponential harvest in future generations. I don't know. Those parts of the story have yet to be written.

Each of us has a purpose in the bigger picture, and it is very possible that the generational sowing and generational blessings

GENERATIONAL
BLESSINGS—
BOTH THE
SOWING AND THE
REAPING—ARE
NOT CONFINED
TO A BIOLOGICAL
OR LEGAL
FRAMEWORK

are beyond the family we currently see or belong to. While I am not directly in Amanda or Anne's line of natural blessing, I have been blessed by watching them and learning from them. While I was not in Dave Thomas' immediate family, I have been blessed by the work he started. God's bigger family shares in the blessings of its individual members. Generational blessings—both the sowing and the reaping—are not confined to a biological or legal framework.

ENDNOTES

1. https://web.archive.org/web/20070628165205/http://www.wendys.com/dave/davethomas_biography.pdf
2. Lancaster Online 10/17/2012.

Chapter 20
L.E.G.A.C.Y.

When I was 38, my mother's older brother passed away at the relatively young age of 65. My uncle was someone I admired. He had been a very successful businessman. He had been active and healthy. He would ski mountains I would never even consider tackling in my wildest dreams. Less than a year before his death, his doctor described his heart as that of a person considerably younger, yet here he was in a casket. My son, Joshua, was just a few months old when I last saw my uncle in hospice, barely recognizable as the man I had remembered. Realistically, my uncle should have lived to see Joshua graduate from college. My uncle did not have any children and had enjoyed a very comfortable lifestyle and lavish vacations. In his final months, he stopped eating and resorted to consuming little more than alcohol. Part of me wonders if at the root of his death was giving up on life. Was he struggling to see that his life had mattered for anything beyond himself? Did he not see a legacy that would live on beyond him? His death gave me a lot to think about.

At age 39, I started having a midlife crisis. As I evaluated my strong reaction to the approaching milestone birthday, I thought about the goals that I had not yet finished and others that I had not yet started. Some I could cross off the list because in the grand scheme of things, they just weren't that important to me anymore. Others I would chose to leave on because I saw value in them but it was okay if they weren't done by 40. There was one goal on the list that I just couldn't brush off. The thing that was eating at me more than anything had to do with leaving a legacy. Would there be something significant that would live on beyond me?

God wired me as a giver, so I had always wanted to start a foundation by age 40. While that may have been my plan, God had not yet opted to bless me in a way that would make a personal foundation an economically viable option. I was determined to find whatever the next best option would be. The core goal was to leave a philanthropic legacy. After considerable searching, I was able to find viable alternatives at my local community foundation. I could structure a legacy giving plan even if I didn't have massive amounts of money to give. I could do the same things as major local philanthropic leaders just on a smaller scale.

One day I was asked to be part of a team of special dinner hosts and hostesses who would share their stories in an effort to inspire others. I needed to come up with something that could sum up why I do the things I do in a way that would convey my heart without coming off as too "religious" and potentially discounting the validity or sincerity of my words for any listeners who were coming at this from a secular perspective. At the core my goal is furthering the kingdom, but I felt I needed a more superficial spin.

As I was driving to work one morning it came to me ... L.E.G.A.C.Y.
... Leaving an Everlasting Gift to Affect Change in Youth.

So much of what I had already done in my adult life fell under that umbrella. Being pro-life and serving on a board was about saving the lives of babies and helping change the destiny of teenage moms. Choosing adoption was choosing to affect the destiny of Mila and Navo. Choosing to work with the community foundation was about choosing to financially support the future of Christian education and athletics which have been so influential for my children.

A picture of a young boy with the words PRIORITIES has been prominent in my house since college. It has this quote: "A hundred years from now it will not matter what my bank account was, the sort of house I lived in, or the kind of car I drove, but the world may be different because I was important in the life of a child" (Forest E Witcraft). When I first put that picture up, I don't think I realized just how meaningful, and perhaps prophetic, it was. The choices I've made haven't always been easy but hopefully one hundred years from now future generations will have been blessed because of those choices.

The concept of passing legacy as it relates to parenting has been very different between my adopted children and natural children. Mila and Navo arrived when they were halfway to adulthood. The years of parenting them were more about undoing damage from the challenges of the past and getting them on a path toward success. In addition, I was younger and my head wasn't yet in the place of thinking about passing legacy torches. Much more of my activities were centered on current needs and character development.

With my natural children, I've had the opportunity to start with clean slates and guide them from day one. Hopefully, I've done more right than wrong. I am older and have a different perspective. I am much more interested in equipping them to carry the legacy torch that I will someday pass. I am very interested in identifying the causes that they may be passionate about. Those passions may be related to the call of God on their life, and I want to equip them to excel within that call. I have noticed, at least with the first two who've gotten to this point, that between ages 9 and 11, their God-given passion for a certain cause seems to emerge.

I enjoy volunteering and serving, much like I saw my grandmother do. At times, my children have no choice but to come along. At other times, they are simply stuck as I make an impromptu decision to do some volunteering when I see help is needed with cleanup or teardown after an event. Lots of hands make light work and our family has a whole lot of hands! Usually, there is something helpful I can find for them to do even if it is just holding a door or picking up some trash on the ground. I want them to internalize the idea that if you see a need and have the ability to meet it, you just do it.

An older couple was living across the street when we moved in. When Mila and Navo were still at home, they knew it was just our standard operating procedure to go shovel snow for them.

The husband passed away. If we could get to it before one of their sons did, we would shovel the snow. The wife has now passed away so one of the sons will be living in the house. I'm still younger than him, and as I write this, Lydia and Caleb are now at a point where they can actively help also. I want my children to honor the older generations and this is one simple tangible way to do that. I don't live near some of my aging relatives, so serving them isn't easy. I will gladly sow seeds by helping someone else's aging relative and perhaps will reap the harvest of someone else helping my own aging relatives.

Mila and Navo have moved on to adult life, and it's been encouraging to see what they've done with what they've learned. Even though they weren't naturally born into the heritage of service, the heritage is still being passed down. They've both chosen careers of service to our nation, but service has also entered into play in the choice to volunteer. In December 2013, I got to have one of those really proud mom moments. Navo was deployed on a Navy guided missile cruiser in the Mediterranean, and often we didn't know exactly where he was or what he was doing because of security. An article appeared in the military news, the Malta Embassy website, and then the *Malta Times*. There was a picture of Navo washing windows as part of the Navy's volunteer team. Here was my little boy, grown up, and doing good things on an international stage.

The USS Monterey (CG 61) recently returned to Malta, enabling its crew to experience the rich culture and history of the island. In keeping with the US Navy's policy of being ambassadors in all areas of the world, 23 volunteers from the Monterey lent a helping hand at Dar tal-Providenza in Siġġiewi. The volunteers and ship's chaplain met with Fr Martin Micallef, director of the home, and residents and then conducted a number of activities. The crew members carried out general maintenance and cleaning in the laundry, kitchen, the seamstress' premises and the chapel area. Monterey is deployed in support of maritime security operations and theatre security cooperation efforts in the US 6th Fleet area of operations.[1]

One day, I was running errands with my young children. We happened to see a gentleman standing at an intersection near a shopping center. He was holding a cardboard sign which my daughter proceeded to read. She then asked about homelessness. I gave a basic response but then had a choice to make. I could try to answer all of her questions or I could opt for something significantly more creative. What if I reached out to the local Christian organization that runs a homeless shelter? Perhaps I could find someone who could speak with authority on the topic and could inspire my children in a way I could not.

The organization was open to the idea, so I took all of my children to the local shelter for a tour and to get advice on the best ways to help a homeless person. Surely those who work with this population daily would have sage advice. My children responded well to the experience and later that day, as we were exiting the highway, we came to the top of the ramp where there was a man standing along the road holding his cardboard sign. We happened to have a cooler of water in the back of our van, and I had one of the children reach back and grab a bottle. I rolled down the window and handed it to him as we proceeded on our way. One of the suggestions that had been given to us earlier that day was rather than giving cash to give something practical like food or a cold drink. My children were struck by the timing of having just learned what to do that morning, then seeing this man and "just so happening" to have the water with us so we could act on what we had learned. God definitely orchestrated that sequence of events perfectly.

Shortly after that, my daughter started asking questions about overseas orphanages. Once again, I had a choice to give answers from my database of knowledge or look for something a little more impactful. I called the director of a local ministry and asked to have my daughter meet with her. This director was once an orphan herself. What better person to answer questions than someone who knows the answers from firsthand experience? Before going to her office, I had my daughter compile a list of questions. I chose not to filter them. They were her honest questions. It was obvious that she had no idea about the plight of orphans in third world countries and that was okay. The conversation was going to take her way outside of her suburban middle-class world. It may shock her and evoke emotions, but I felt she could handle it.

The director pulled out books of pictures and spoke of her experiences. She spoke of the vision of their ministry and the actions they are taking to impact orphans around the world. She explained about the number of orphans being similar to the number of mailboxes in the US and challenged Lydia to count mailboxes on our way home. One hour and one hundred mailboxes later, my daughter had a strong heart for orphans. I could have talked about orphans for hours and never had the

> THERE ARE TIMES IN PARENTING WHERE THE BEST ANSWERS OR INFLUENCES FOR YOUR CHILD COME FROM SOMEONE ELSE

impact on her that this woman had. There are times in parenting where the best answers or influences for your child come from someone else.

In Lydia's case, her passion for orphans came out after she asked specific questions and I sought out creative answers. In the case of my son, Caleb, things began emerging as an outgrowth of the stuff we were already doing. One of the fun volunteer things we've found to do as a family is packing food with Feed My Starving Children MobilePack events. It's a simple way for the children to do something tangible to make a difference. Children can put stickers on bags. They can pour rice, soy, veggies, and vitamins into a funnel. They can hold bags under a funnel. They can learn to add or take out rice to adjust the bags to proper weights. They can press a handle down on a sealer. They can line up bags to accumulate the correct number for a box. Volunteering can be fun, and we have genuinely had fun at the MobilePack events. We have had so much fun that we've been known to make mini mission trips of MobilePacks. A mission trip involving airlines, vaccinations, time off from work or school, etc. would be difficult and costly for a family like ours, but piling the family into a minivan on a weekend to go serve an hour or two from home is relatively easy.

Caleb's passion is emerging in the area of helping the homeless and hungry. He has specifically asked for me to look for opportunities where he can serve. He does not need to wait until he is much older to move into these passions if they are, in fact, part of the call God has on his life. I found another local food outreach program that is an extension from our church and love that the man in charge of the outreaches takes the time to encourage Caleb and speak into his life. If we happen to see Edgar at church, he will specifically call Caleb out by name. Edgar has natural children, including his own Caleb, who are not that much older than our Caleb and he understands the mentoring and fathering heart. The fact that they both seem to share some of the same giftings and passions means he can influence Caleb in a way that I cannot. This volunteering is much more about encouraging Caleb in his passion and mom tagging along. For now we serve together, but someday Caleb will be an adult and will serve without me.

Helping children grow in their passion definitely requires effort and intentionality. I have to be constantly on the lookout for opportunities to expose them to what's happening out there in the world and eventually in their specific field of interest. Men and women with similar gifts and interests can speak into their lives in ways I cannot, so I need to be constantly on alert for opportunities to cross paths with these men and women. Sometimes the exposure is face to face, and other times it is sharing their book or a video about them. There are torches that these men and women will eventually need to pass to another member of the body of Christ and perhaps one of my children will be the one to whom the torch is passed.

Dedicate your children to God and point them in the way that they should go, and the values they've learned from you will be with them for life.

PROVERBS 22:6 TPT

ENDNOTE

1. https://timesofmalta.com/articles/view/USS-Monterey-reciprocates-Maltese-hospitality.502344.

Chapter 21
Creative Custom Designed Parenting

I remember my mother being concerned that my brother and I would not know what a healthy two-parent family looks like because we didn't grow up in one. When I was young, there was a summer when my mother dropped my brother and me off at the farm of family friends while she went to work. They were a solid Christian family. Mom and dad had a solid marriage and good parenting skills. I can honestly say that even as a young child there were good things I watched and remembered about their relationship and their parenting. I'm far from a perfect parent but every once in a while, I will nail it. Some of those really good parenting moments have been heavily influenced by that couple.

Each of my children, adopted or natural, is unique. Figuring out how to reach each one has been an adventure. Unfortunately, what works for one child doesn't necessarily work for the next child.

When Mila and Navo arrived, they had to learn new ways of viewing the world and personal responsibility. The first change was that I would be packing lunches for them. They were accustomed to the idea that they got lunches for "free" at school. They didn't understand that the "free" lunches weren't really "free," but subsidized based on need. We would not qualify for the "free" lunches. We were part of the group of taxpayers helping pay for the lunches.

> THEY DIDN'T UNDERSTAND THAT CHOOSING TO HAVE ONE THING MAY MEAN CHOOSING TO NOT HAVE SOMETHING ELSE.

They were struggling with the idea that in their new home, the adults in the house went to work every day. They didn't understand why. They had moved around a lot in their short lives and lived with lots of different people. There were times that they saw adults not going to work, yet somehow there was still a place to live and food to eat. They assumed things were free and money just came in the mail. They didn't understand how much things cost or how choices were made. They didn't understand that choosing to have one thing may mean choosing to not have something else.

One day, I got a little creative to try to make a point. I pulled out the Monopoly money and crafted some lessons in how things work in real life. I explained that when you go to work you get paid for doing a job for your employer. I told them they had done a good job at work and handed them some money. I then asked them if they liked having a room to sleep in. They naturally said yes, and I told them that's called paying the rent or the mortgage and they would need to give me some of their money. I then asked if they like to eat. I explained that the grocery store wanted money for the food that we picked out and again they had to relinquish some of the money in their hands. I then asked if they liked being able to turn the lights on. They were catching on to the pattern and turned over money to pay for electric. To make this stick in the head of a little boy, I then asked if they liked being able to flush the toilet. After the giggles, more money was relinquished to pay for the water and sewer bill. Before long, they were out of their Monopoly money. I then noted that we hadn't talked about going to McDonalds or the toy store. They quickly realized that money eventually runs out so sometimes we don't get everything we want. They also realized that the only way they would get more money was to go to work.

I was feeling pretty good that they got the message, and then Navo piped up that the game was fun. Let's play again. Maybe it didn't quite work as planned but it was a start. During the second round, we introduced another life lesson. I sent them to pick out a die-cast car from the cabinet that held my husband's collection. I don't remember any longer what make and model they each picked out, but I remember one being significantly more costly than the other, so I was able to illustrate the impact to the budget of the fancy expensive car vs. the practical, less expensive car. In the game, one of my children had to now sleep in the fancy expensive car because there was no money left to pay for housing.

During that first year, there were lots of life lessons to be learned. Every morning, I would drop the children off in front of the elementary school in the city. They would hang out on the playground with the other children until the bell rang. One day, I was at the office, and around lunchtime, the principal called me.

Apparently, Navo had just showed up at school. I was immediately asking questions because I had dropped him off four hours earlier. If he was not in the classroom then where in the world had he been, and if he wasn't in school for the last four hours, what about Mila? Mila had been in class, but apparently, Navo and a few other boys had wandered off the playground and down the hill to a vacant old building behind the school. They were tossing rocks up at the windows. Oh boy, I was going to be having some interesting conversations over dinner that night! That evening we talked about how those were not good choices. During the conversation, Navo explained how it didn't matter because it wasn't anyone's building. I now had to reorient his understanding of ownership and inhabitation. I asked him about the prior house he lived in. Who owned that? He knew that was his new dad's house. He agreed that yes, we owned it, even though at the time no one was living in it. He agreed that we wouldn't want people throwing rocks at it. He now realized that just because no one is in a building doesn't mean someone doesn't own it. Fortunately, we never had that problem again, or at least not that I know of.

I WAS GOING TO BE HAVING SOME INTERESTING CONVERSATIONS OVER DINNER THAT NIGHT.

When we switched Mila and Navo to the Christian school, we were well on our way to academic progress. Because it was a small school, we got to know the teachers and the teachers got to know us. Navo started off one of his years with a teacher who was very new to her teaching career. It wasn't long before he was testing his limits on math homework. Math was just not his thing. Being a working mom has always made it tough for me to keep up with every detail of daily school things. There isn't much time after getting home from work, getting dinner on the table, cleaning up, etc. to chase down every detail. When I was young, my brother and I were latch-key children. We were home two hours before mom got home, and we did our homework on our own during that time. I had just sort of fallen into the pattern that I saw modeled. This brand new teacher realized she was going to have to contact Navo's parents about the homework. She was understandably nervous about sending one of her first emails to a parent about a problem with their child. She pushed send on the email and headed to her lunch break. The topic came up with another teacher over lunch. That teacher knew me and assured her not to worry. In fact, there was a good chance she would be amused with the response. I read the email and crafted one of my classic responses:

> "So, young Mr. Rosado deems it wise to skip doing his math homework. We will be sure to have a discussion about that this evening. Just so we are on the same page, should he ever tell you that there is no one at home who can help him with his math homework, feel free to call him on it. While I didn't enjoy it, I somehow survived two years of calculus and it is highly unlikely that he is going to bring anything home that I can't help figure out."

My children learned pretty quickly not to play too many games with their teachers. I've been pretty picky about the schools I've chosen for my children and tend to be on the same page with their teachers.

As a teenager, Navo once pulled a stunt that was getting a little too close to potential legal trouble for him. I reached out to my brother's friend who works in the juvenile probation system. We also reached out to my husband's old high school acquaintance who works for the city police department. We landed on a plan to "scare him straight." We alerted the school to our plan, and they were willing to go along with it. We showed up in the middle of the day, picked him up, and took him down to the city police station where my husband's acquaintance gave him the straight scoop on what could happen if he tried a stunt like that again. He showed him a holding cell complete with the toilet in the corner. We never had another problem like that again. As I type this, I wonder if that might have had the unintended consequence of planting a seed for his future career in his mind. He currently serves in a military police role for the US Navy.

Sometimes parenting has involved considerably less weighty approaches to getting a child's attention to encourage a change in behavior. I have been known to imitate a child's tantrum to show just how silly and ridiculous they look. When they see me, they can't help but laugh and the tantrum ends. It can be a balancing act. I generally know (or maybe it's just some good old-fashioned Holy Spirit wisdom helping me know) when I can use the sarcastic humor versus a more sensitive approach.

Mila was my first adventure into how to connect with a child, particularly a teenager. I remember there were times when I simply had to sit with her, wherever that might be, even if it meant crawling into a closet to be next to her. Out of the box techniques like that I chalk up to Holy Spirit nudges when I needed them.

I've heard Rick Yancey quoted many times over the years. "God doesn't call the equipped. God equips the called." I definitely wasn't equipped to parent children when I was called, literally. God equipped me along the way. If you are called to parent children—fostered, adopted, natural, step, whatever—God will equip you along the way if you allow Him.

> *"May he [God] work perfection into every part of you*
> *giving you all that you need to fulfill your destiny.*
>
> HEBREWS 13:21A TPT

"GOD DOESN'T CALL
THE EQUIPPED.
GOD EQUIPS
THE CALLED."

RICK YANCEY

Chapter 22
Encouraging the Warrior Spirit

Finally, be strong in the Lord and in his mighty power. Put on the full armor of God, so that you can take your stand against the devil's schemes. For our struggle is not against flesh and blood, but against the rulers, against the authorities, against the powers of this dark world and against the spiritual forces of evil in the heavenly realms. Therefore put on the full armor of God, so that when the day of evil comes, you may be able to stand your ground, and after you have done everything, to stand. Stand firm then, with the belt of truth buckled around your waist, with the breastplate of righteousness in place, and with your feet fitted with the readiness that comes from the gospel of peace. In addition to all this, take up the shield of faith, with

which you can extinguish all the flaming arrows of the
evil one. Take the helmet of salvation and the sword of
the Spirit, which is the word of God.

EPHESIANS 6:10-17

We live in a fallen world, and every day there are opportunities to be a victim or to take up our rightful position as overcoming warriors. We are surrounded by people who are under attack and feeling burdened. Our adversary may look like the person in front of us but the Bible points to the real adversary being the liar deceiving them. We can lock arms and fight the good fight with them or we can stand by and watch them struggle. What if each morning we arose with an unshakeable conviction that the warrior spirit within was going to be on duty?

Nature can give us great examples to grasp spiritual truth. When I remember back to the warrior spirit rising up in me on behalf of Mila, I think of a dog with a bone. If the dog really wants the bone, it doesn't matter how much you try to yank it away from him. You may end up moving the whole dog but you won't get that bone. The situation with Mila was yanking me all over the place but I was holding on to the truth that Jesus would heal her.

You could try holding something else out for the dog with the bone but if the dog wants to hold on to the bone, the dog is going to ignore whatever else you have. Once I felt I had my God-given mandate, I wasn't going to release my grip on the truth. I wasn't going to waste my time arguing with anyone on how I might not see the answer to my prayer in the way I wanted to see it. The inpatient programs and medications were the counterfeits and I wasn't letting go of the truth I now had. Allowing that righteous stubbornness to bubble up from the depths of who I am carried me through that season of seemingly endless battles.

There may be times that God calls you to do battle on behalf of another person or situation. You may or may not get to see clearly on this side of Heaven the impact of your obedience, but don't let that stop you. On a few occasions I've felt called into someone else's battle. One particular one sticks out in my memory.

YOU MAY OR MAY NOT GET TO SEE CLEARLY ON THIS SIDE OF HEAVEN THE IMPACT OF YOUR OBEDIENCE, BUT DON'T LET THAT STOP YOU

One day, I was riding in a vehicle and got an overwhelming sense that there was a significant battle going on between light and darkness or good and evil in a particular situation. My spirit was sensing a very strong and important battle. I knew some of the players in the natural situation but was really only on the periphery. I couldn't shake the feeling, and though I didn't know exactly what was happening in the natural, I allowed the warrior in me to go on the offensive.

The next morning I woke up with the sense that I should call in reinforcements and specific people came to mind because of their physical proximity to the natural situation and because of their capacity to pray with great spiritual authority. It felt strange to be asking for people to pray fervently about a situation when I wasn't really sure why. Later that day, I was brought into the natural situation, still very much unsure of why I was being so burdened. "Okay, Lord, why am I here? What am I supposed to be doing?" As I stood there, I suddenly became keenly aware that my call to action was because the Gospel was to be presented in the situation and behind the scenes there was a very serious battle underway that threatened to prevent it.

In the natural, I was there to speak up and help pave the way for the person who was to present the Gospel. In the supernatural, I was there to battle any spirit of darkness that would prevent the Gospel from having a clear path. As I left the natural situation that day, I had a clear sense of peace that I had done what I was to do. I then reached back out to the reinforcements sharing with them exactly what had happened. It was definitely encouraging that day to have the natural mind seeing and understanding what was happening in the supernatural. My spiritual boldness moved up another notch.

Sometimes the warrior spirit needs some external encouragement and music can be a powerful tool. As I was standing in faith on Mila's behalf one of my favorite songs became Carman's Satan, Bite the Dust. The music and the accompanying video are set in the style of a country-western bar fight. Carman walks in like the town sheriff carrying the warrant for Satan's arrest. With aggressive bold spiritual authority he stands up to the demons in the bar and exercises his authority over them. Carman is theatrically portraying the essence of a warrior spirit engaged in a spiritual battle.

Carman's passion and showmanship can't help but to fire up faith. Songs like *Revival in the Land, We Need God in America Again,* and *R.I.O.T* (Righteous Invasion Of Truth) are timeless.

One day when Mila was going through her struggles, she heard the Rich Mullins and Rich McVicker song *My Deliverer*. She loved the song, and it became one she played often. Jesus became her Deliverer and the song was reinforcing her faith in that truth.

A more recent song I have found particularly encouraging is *Do It Again* performed by Elevation Worship (among others). Having experienced the miracles of walking through adoption, loss, and natural children I know God hasn't failed me. I couldn't always see it while walking through it but hindsight is 20/20. I've seen God move mountains, and because of that, I believe He can do the same for others. I can empathize with those walking through loss and believe with them for future successes.

YOU MAY OR MAY
NOT GET TO SEE
CLEARLY ON THIS
SIDE OF HEAVEN
THE IMPACT OF
YOUR OBEDIENCE,
BUT DON'T LET
THAT STOP YOU

Chapter 23
The Heavenly Strategy Game

⸻

Most of the time in my daily life, I see things in the natural realm separate from anything supernatural. At other times, the natural seems to fade into the background and I see the supernatural. Every once in a while, I see both the natural and supernatural realms simultaneously, and occasionally, it is in seemingly every day, ordinary events.

One evening as I was leaving work, I remembered I needed to pick up something at Walmart. I drove over, parked my car, walked in the store, bought what I needed, and headed back toward my car. I "just so happened" to be at the right place, at the right time, to be part of something just a little bit bigger than me.

As I was walking to my car, I noticed a woman had come out with her fairly loaded shopping cart. She was putting things in the trunk of the car, but had also opened the driver's door and tried to start the car. I'm far from an expert in automotive things, but the engine wasn't turning over, and it sounded like the battery was too weak. I had encountered similar problems in the past with various vehicles we own. I "just so happened" to have a set of really good, extra-long jumper cables in the trunk of my car which was parked just a few spaces past her.

There was another couple who "just so happened" to have walked out moments ahead of me who were heading to the same area of the parking lot and had also observed the woman struggling to start the car. They had a larger SUV with a really strong battery and were parked just a few spaces away.

It was as if a dance was taking place and everyone knew the steps. There was no real discussion of a plan or even discussion about the woman's need. I walked to my car and retrieved the jumper cables. The other couple brought over their vehicle. The gentleman stepped into action hooking up the cables to the two vehicles, and with one turn of the key, the engine started. In almost the same fluid motion as it came together, the cables were disconnected and everyone went on their way.

As I was driving home, I saw the sequence of events replayed on another level. It was as if I was having the opportunity to be a "fly on the wall" in heaven watching God and the angels sitting around a table moving pieces on a chess board. I imagined God saying, "Hey guys, see that lady over there in Aisle 6 at Walmart? She's getting a bunch of stuff and her car is going to present a problem. She recently observed people stuck on the side of the road with car troubles and fears that ever happening to her. Watch what I'm going to do! Yo, H.S., can you give that couple coming into the parking lot one of your little nudges to park over there in that empty space, and can you remind Cathie she needs to swing by the store."

"Got it boss," the Holy Spirit responds and heads off to do his work.

Angel Gabriel asks "Do you need us to do anything?"

God responds, "No, we've got this one covered."

The angels watch as everyone does what they are doing and gradually move into position. The Holy Spirit is on alert in case anyone needs an extra nudge to do what they are supposed to do, or if He has to go to Plan B and bring in a backup when the planned players aren't obedient. God already knows how the situation is going to play out and begins announcing the play by play as if announcing for a sporting event.

> THE HOLY SPIRIT IS ON ALERT IN CASE ANYONE NEEDS AN EXTRA NUDGE TO DO WHAT THEY ARE SUPPOSED TO DO.

(I have no idea of the names of all of the actual people involved in this story, so I'll just make some up.) Sue is walking out of the store to her car. She opens the car door and puts the key into the ignition to get it started, presumably, so it can cool off inside while she loads the groceries. The car appears to have a problem. Sue doesn't seem to know what to do. It looks like she's going to just go ahead and put the groceries in the trunk. Maybe she hopes the car will miraculously turn over the next time she turns the key. Here comes Bob and Bonnie. Bonnie seems to have noticed Sue's car trouble and is saying something to Bob. Cathie is right behind Bob and Bonnie and also seems to be noticing the situation.

It sounds like Bonnie just told Sue they'll get their SUV. I think Cathie just signaled she'll get the jumper cables. Sue is starting to look a little less stressed as she's putting the last of the bags in the trunk of the car. Here comes Cathie with a set of jumper cables. Bob and Bonnie are pulling up. Bob pops the hood on the SUV. Cathie hands Bob the cables. Sue pops the hood on her car. Bob hooks up the cables and signals to Sue to turn the key. The car starts. Cathie, Bonnie, and Bob share a moment of victory. Sue says thank you. Bob unhooks the cables and hands them to Cathie. He closes the hood on Sue's car and their SUV. Bob and Bonnie drive away. Cathie says a few words to Sue and drives away. Sue also drives away, amazed at the kindness of strangers to aid her in her plight.

Gabriel gives God and the Holy Spirit a high five. "Good game, well played. Everyone did what they were supposed to do, and I like how you had the answer to Sue's prayer in the works before she even knew she needed one."

As I reflected on that seemingly inconsequential little sequence of events, I was struck with how everything had lined up in such perfectly synchronized motion. It wasn't profound. It wasn't that eventful. It wasn't super spiritual. It was simply people going about their everyday lives, but seeing a need right in front of them and choosing to offer up whatever they had to meet it. On another level, I wondered if it was really part of something even bigger.

> I WAS STRUCK WITH HOW EVERYTHING HAD LINED UP IN SUCH PERFECTLY SYNCHRONIZED MOTION

That little sequence of events is just one part of a bigger sequence of events in the lives of each of the people involved. I can guarantee each person took something different away from that encounter. It could be as simple as, "I did my good deed of the day," or as important as, "God really is watching out for me and will take care of me." I don't know what else may have been going on in Sue's life. I don't know what her relationship was at that moment with the Lord and didn't feel I was being directed to go get into a long spiritual discussion. Perhaps that seemingly inconsequential set of events is part of God's bigger relentless pursuit of Sue. I may never know until I get to heaven.

In Luke 15:4-7 Jesus told a parable to the people who had gathered together to hear him. "Suppose one of you has a hundred sheep and loses one of them. Doesn't he leave the ninety-nine in the open country and go after the lost sheep until he finds it? And when he finds it, he joyfully puts it on his shoulders and goes home. Then he calls his friends and neighbors together and says, 'Rejoice with me; I have found my lost sheep.' I tell you that in the same way there will be more rejoicing in heaven over one sinner who repents than over ninety-nine righteous persons who do not need to repent."

When God goes after a lost sheep, He'll stop at nothing. He may even orchestrate little encounters at a Walmart to show His love. I'm convinced that nothing really happens by chance, it's just we may not see the entire bigger picture. Yes, I may have seen this little event from a slightly higher perspective than normal, but someday in heaven I hope to see the even bigger picture.

The bigger picture can take a while to come together. In 2 Peter 3: 8-9 it says this: "But do not forget this one thing, dear friends: With the Lord a day is like a thousand years, and a thousand years are like a day. The Lord is not slow in keeping his promise, as some understand slowness. Instead he is patient with you, not wanting anyone to perish, but everyone to come to repentance."

When I think back over the story of my life that has been written thus far, I am reminded of how long things can take to come to fruition. The seeds and foreshadowing of adoption were there at my childhood home but it would be more than 20 years until I had two children in my home and chose to adopt them. God knew the circumstances under which they would be born and the stuff they would go through before coming to me. He knew what things I needed to experience and things I would need to learn before He could bring them into my life. Part of God's plan to relentlessly pursue and ultimately retrieve the lost sheep of Mila and Navo was to bring them into my life. I was just a piece of their bigger picture.

God knew the impact seeing the babies in the NICU had on me in my mid-20s. He knew I wanted to help. He did not forget that desire. He simply chose to answer it in His timing and in a way that was way bigger than my mind could have ever grasped. Perhaps someday in heaven I will meet a mother or child who was impacted by my choice to be a donor mom and thus was part of their bigger picture.

God put heroes in my path who would have interesting parallels to my story and would reinforce that often it is through our pain that purpose and passion are found. God knew that I would lose children to miscarriage. That isn't His perfect plan but something that happens because we live in a fallen world. I know those children are in Heaven and I will see them again. There have been times when I've wrestled with whether I wish God would have done things differently, but I can't deny that He's allowed good to come out of those dark places. I can truly empathize with women who walk a similar road and be part of their bigger picture.

> WE MAY NOT ALWAYS UNDERSTAND HIS TIMING AND IT MAY SEEM LONG AND SLOW, BUT THE BOTTOM LINE IS HE DOES KEEP HIS PROMISES

God has blessed me with four natural children whom I get to parent on earth. God knows the plans and purpose for their lives and has allowed me to be a piece of their bigger picture and the bigger picture they will be for other people.

We may not always understand his timing and it may seem long and slow, but the bottom line is this—He does keep His promises. The answers may not always look like what we had planned, but it is all part of His bigger plan. The bigger plan is He doesn't want anyone to perish without knowing Him. When Wendy Walters opened the Release the Writer conference, she quoted Revelation 12:11, "We overcome by the blood of the Lamb and the word of our testimony." Maybe part of the bigger picture was for me to go through all of those life experiences to write a book that you read and helps you realize just how much He loves you and has been pursuing you. He leaves the ninety-nine to pursue the one. If you are that one, He wants to adopt you and say welcome home. He has chosen you as His Plan A.

THE END

Appendix A
Discussion Questions

1. What influences from your childhood became invaluable later in life or helped you navigate your way to your destiny?

2. Are there any things that you were passionate about on a surface level that later became part of your destiny?

3. What were your dreams that perhaps didn't come true or not in the way you would have expected but in hindsight you would not change?

4. Have you ever had a moment or season when the warrior spirit rose up in you and your faith carried you through something you never thought possible?

5. Has there ever been a time in your life where God put you on a path to take a non-traditional route to learn life lessons before you could accomplish an end goal?

6. Have you ever had an area of life where you had to reprogram your own thinking from "I can't" to "I can?"

7. Do you have a God story where He spoke directly to your heart whether through images, people, sounds, smells, etc.?

8. Have you ever faced a seemingly impossible situation and how did you get to the other side?

9. God is the Redeemer of lives but also redeems situations, dates, places, etc. Describe how God redeemed something in your life.

10. God sometimes seems to take his time answering certain prayers. Describe a time where he answered a prayer, perhaps in a totally unexpected way or after what seemed like forever.

11. Have you ever faced a situation that challenged you to the core and you had to sort out your own heart issues before you could invite others into your situation?

12. What is the meaning of your name and how have you seen God bring that out in your life?

13. Have you ever struggled with accepting God's truth about yourself and how did you finally work through that struggle?

14. How many children do you have?

15. Describe an event where it was undeniable that God was doing a miracle to give you a platform to demonstrate his love or greatness.

16. Who do you consider to be your heroes and why?

17. What generational blessings or legacies are you a part of?

18. What is your passion? How did you find it and grow in it?

19. Describe a situation that required creative, out of the box, Holy Spirit inspired parenting.

20. What encourages your warrior spirit?

21. Describe a time when you experienced the natural and supernatural worlds colliding.

Appendix B
New to Jesus?

If you prayed the prayer in Chapter 16 to accept Jesus into your heart or if you have more questions about beginning that relationship that adopts you into God's family, here are some resources and recommendations.

- PeaceWithGod.net
- 1-800-Need Him (1-800-633-3446) or Needhim.org/knowing-Jesus/
- ChatAboutJesus.com

I recommend starting to read (or listen to) the Bible. There are so many different translations available to those of us in the English world. I happen to have a very worn leather-bound New American Standard, but I also like the newer Passion translation. My children have often used the New King James version in school. I honestly have quite a collection of translations that I have amassed over the years when I found different translations available in very inexpensive paperbacks. Today I can go online and find almost any translation I want to read in a free online format.

Where to start reading in the Bible?

You can start at the beginning like a traditional book, but there is truth and wisdom everywhere, so don't feel like you have to start at the beginning. I've often heard the recommendation for a brand new person to start with the book of John (in the New Testament, right after Matthew, Mark, and Luke). You could also read a chapter of Proverbs each day (in the Old Testament right after Psalms). It is loaded with simple, practical advice for life.

What about finding a church?

I consider myself a denominational mutt. I mentioned the Episcopal heritage but was baptized Catholic as a baby. I accepted Jesus in a Child Evangelism Fellowship Good News Club at a Methodist church when I was an early elementary student. I spent many years in a non-denominational church heavily influenced by charismatic and Amish roots, went off to college, and attended a Presbyterian church with friends after a period of wayward wandering. When I moved back to Lancaster County, I went with friends to various places, from the Church of the Brethren to Assemblies of God. I joined the staff of the Assemblies of God church and had my wedding there. After the church split, I returned to my non-denominational roots. Today I have friends and serve alongside brothers and sisters in Christ who attend Plain, Mennonite, Catholic, and many other

Protestant denominational and non-denominational churches. The label on the sign outside is more about style and less about your relationship with Jesus.

I would tell you to find a church where you are comfortable, but that's not exactly right. To grow, you need a place with a mix of comfortable "Amen" sermons and "Oh me" sermons that aren't necessarily comfortable. You will need people around you to encourage you, challenge you,

THE LABEL ON THE SIGN OUTSIDE IS MORE ABOUT STYLE AND LESS ABOUT YOUR RELATIONSHIP WITH JESUS

and hold you accountable. I'm not a fan of hopping around from church to church, although you may do that while you find the right fit. Your personality may mean you feel more comfortable in one style or another, and that is fine: small or large, pipe organ or electric guitars and drums, hymnals or modern choruses on a screen, pews or chairs, ornate old building or modern building or converted gymnasium or even a home—as long as the gathering is centered in Jesus!

You may land at a church for a season and then eventually move on because it no longer feels right. I've come to realize that just as people have different callings, churches have different callings. I grew up in a church with a very heavy emphasis on missions. I am grateful for that foundation being instilled in me. When my young natural children came along, getting three children age four and under ready and out the door to a church 30 minutes away became a bit of a challenge. We moved to a church closer to our home. After a while, I started feeling like it wasn't the right place for us. There was nothing wrong with the church itself, but I couldn't shake an internal friction and frustration. In hindsight, I can clearly see how God needed our family to move to a new place to be influenced by new people to move us forward for the next season. You may find after a season at a church that you feel it is time to move on. There is no need to burn bridges; just move on graciously. These are still your brothers and sisters in Christ. Simply recognize that God uses different churches to meet the needs of different people and accomplish different purposes in different seasons. No one church has to be everything for everyone, and we accomplish a lot more when we look past our style differences and work together to love and positively impact people.

IF YOU DECLARE WITH YOUR
MOUTH, "JESUS IS LORD," AND
BELIEVE IN YOUR HEART THAT
GOD RAISED HIM FROM THE
DEAD, YOU WILL BE SAVED.

–ROMANS 10:9

ALL OF GOD'S PEOPLE
ARE ORDINARY PEOPLE
WHO HAVE BEEN MADE
EXTRAORDINARY BY THE
PURPOSE HE HAS GIVEN THEM.

—OSWALD CHAMBERS

Elijah House
www.elijahhouse.org

When I was desperate for help for Mila and someone finally said yes, it was an Elijah House trained team. There are Elijah House trained prayer ministries around the world and from their home office in Idaho they can help you find someone in your area. They also carry a variety of products (books, dvds, etc.) on topics around adoption, healing from trauma, etc.

Bethany Christian Services
www.bethany.org

Bethany Christian Services is a worldwide organization assisting families with social services, adoptions, foster care, etc.

Brittany's Hope
www.brittanyshope.org

Brittany's Hope was where Lydia had her questions about orphans answered and is a source for grants for adoptions of special needs children and international adoptions.

Heartbeat International
www.heartbeatservices.org

Originally written by Jim and Anne Pierson, Loving and Caring resource materials for the pro-life community are now available through Heartbeat International.

Ways to Get Involved and Impact Children

There are many ways you can get involved and make a difference in the lives of children. None of us can do everything, but all of us can do something! Here are a few opportunities for you to impact children.

Compassion International
www.compassion.com

Compassion International is an international child sponsorship program. You can sponsor a child and put a face and a name to your outreach.

World Vision
www.worldvision.org

World Vision is another international child sponsorship program.

Feed My Starving Children
www.fmsc.org

This organization holds mobile food packing events around the country and is one of our favorite volunteer activities.

Mom's House
www.momshouse.org

Mom's House is the childcare center where God planted the seed for adoption in me. They are God-centered, nonprofit, licensed childcare centers supporting single parents as they complete their education, find employment, and get off welfare. There are currently seven houses in four states.

Team Orphans
www.teamorphans.com

Our family enjoys participating in Rebecca's Virtual Ironman as a way to support Brittany's Hope while staying active.

Meet the family
Photo Gallery

My great great grandfather, Christian Freck, a member of the 68th Pennsylvania Infantry, Co. F, served at the Battle of Gettysburg.

My maternal great grandparents— Christian's son, Jacob, and his deaf wife, Catherine, for whom I was named.

The young crew on a "family heritage field trip" to visit the Gettysburg Battlefield.

*Family heritage cross—Family lore says Jacob made
this cross that hung on the outside of what used to be
the St. Barnabas Episcopal Church in Burlington, NJ.*

Picture taken in July and Nanny died November— Jacob and Catherine's daughter, my maternal grandmother, Laura Rose at my wedding, only months before she passed and months before she would be taking care of my first child in heaven.

Uncle Bill, with "Nanny" and "Mom." Uncle Bill's passing and the milestone birthday challenged me to think about "L.E.G.A.C.Y."

Little Mila on the left shortly before I put my dress on to walk down the aisle.

Little Navo enjoying potato chips at the wedding reception.

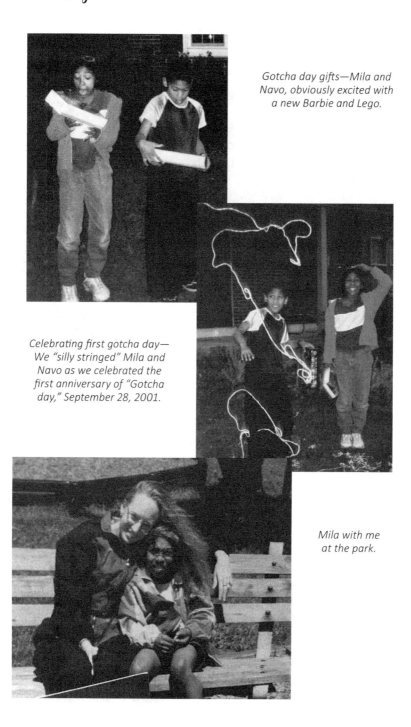

Gotcha day gifts—Mila and Navo, obviously excited with a new Barbie and Lego.

Celebrating first gotcha day— We "silly stringed" Mila and Navo as we celebrated the first anniversary of "Gotcha day," September 28, 2001.

Mila with me at the park.

Mila starting to master the art of being photogenic.

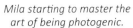

Navo helping paint his new room at the new house and obviously a funny little guy.

Mila and Navo as happy, well-adjusted siblings.

Mila and Navo during the teenage years.

Mila and Navo as young adults.

My dad with little Lydia.

Lydia was destined to walk
early which she did.

The Christian school used
Mila in some advertising.

Mila and Lydia together in Illinois during the last minute surprise of Mila getting permission to fly in from Arizona for Navo's boot camp graduation.

Lydia and Caleb hanging out with a strong and serious Navo.

Mila, Navo, Joshua, Lydia, and Caleb out for an afternoon during boot camp graduation.

Navy man Navo.

Don't mess with this guy
on an aircraft carrier.

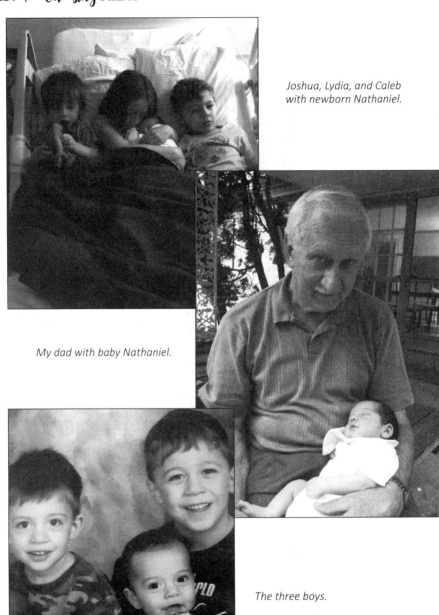

Joshua, Lydia, and Caleb with newborn Nathaniel.

My dad with baby Nathaniel.

The three boys.

*All six of my children on a rare occasion
that they were all in one place at one time.*

*Joshua "helping" pack extra
breastmilk for NICU babies.*

Navo volunteering—making momma very proud!

Delivering Operation Christmas Child Boxes.

*A fun picture after packing food
with Feed My Starving Children.*

*Carrying flags for a fundraising
walk for Brittany's Hope.*

*Mila with Atticus and his first
experience with East Coast snow.*

Marine Mila with her little man.

*Photogenic Mila and Atticus,
like mother like son.*

Nephew Atticus with Uncle Caleb, Aunt Lydia,
Uncle Joshua, and Uncle Nathaniel.

Uncle Nathaniel and Nephew Atticus
—fun mischief in the making!

*Marcello made his entry into the
family just weeks before publishing!*

Meet the Author
Cathie Henry Rosado

———————————————

Cathie Henry Rosado was born in Lancaster County, Pennsylvania, where more than 250 years of her family history is strongly rooted. "Be fruitful and multiply" was very practical advice for this largely agrarian society. Cathie's immediate family would depart from that tradition as her parents met in college and moved toward professional office occupations. She and her younger brother enjoyed a middle-class life, and though their parents divorced, it was amicable, and life was pretty good.

Cathie graduated from a public high school and defied what some saw as odds stacked against her, eventually graduating with a bachelor's of science in economics with a concentration in accounting and entrepreneurial management from the Wharton School of the University of Pennsylvania. She headed into her professional career with many expectations for what life would look like, and then the year 2000 changed everything.

In that one year, she went from being a single professional finishing her Penn State MBA to a married working mother experiencing a whirlwind of change. "Be fruitful and multiply" would not look the same for her as it did for her ancestors. Expectations of how things were going to be would have to be tossed out the window as a whole new adventure lay ahead—one where she would have to keep moving forward even when the steps were difficult or unclear.

Today, Cathie continues to work full time in a professional role while juggling parenting and embracing her passion for volunteering and impacting people. She is trying to figure out her developing grandparent role while the nest is still pretty full. While this book may be her story, the prayer is that it encourages and positively impacts you as you live your story.

Cathie welcomes your feedback and would love to hear from you. To connect with her by email: contact@ChoosingPlanA.com

---

ADOPTION IS
THE VISIBLE
GOSPEL.

–JOHN PIPER

To invite Cathie to speak at your conference or event, visit:

WWW.CHOOSINGPLANA.COM

HOWEVER MOTHERHOOD
COMES TO YOU, IT'S
A MIRACLE.

–VALERIE HARPER

Finished with this book? Please pass it on.

I will not measure the success of this book by the number of copies sold. If just one person finds Jesus or healing because of it, I will consider that success. I may not learn of the book's success until heaven, and I'm okay with that. Just as people have impacted my life, you have the opportunity to impact someone else. When you are finished with this book, I invite you to write an encouraging note and then pass the book to the next person.

Maybe you've heard the audible voice of God saying someone's name, or the Holy Spirit has sent a random name through your mind. I once had a situation where I knew I needed to find a counselor to help someone but had no idea who to call. Suddenly a name popped into my head, but I didn't think it made any sense. I called the woman and explained the situation. She knew exactly why her name came to my mind. I didn't know her whole testimony, and here I was, learning that she could counsel from the unique perspective of personal experience. She was exactly who God wanted to talk to this individual, and she was able to lead the person in a prayer to accept Jesus.

Feel free to share these encouraging notes with me:

contact@ChoosingPlanA.com.

IF THERE'S A CAUSE
WORTH FIGHTING
FOR, IT'S THIS:
CHILDREN BELONG
IN FAMILIES.

–NICOLE SKELLENGER
ADOPTION ADVOCATE
AND ATTORNEY